JESUS,
HOPE DRAWING NEAR

JESUS,
HOPE DRAWING NEAR

Reflections on the Gospels for the C-cycle

Joseph G. Donders

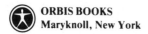 **ORBIS BOOKS**
Maryknoll, New York

 **DOVE COMMUNICATIONS**
Melbourne, Australia

The Catholic Foreign Mission Society of America (Maryknoll) recruits and trains people for overseas missionary service. Through Orbis Books Maryknoll aims to foster the international dialogue that is essential to mission. The books published, however, reflect the opinions of their authors and are not meant to represent the official position of the society.

Library of Congress Cataloging in Publication Data

Donders, Joseph G.
  Jesus, hope drawing near.

  Includes index.
  1. Bible.   N.T.   Gospels—Liturgical lessons,
English—Meditations.   2. Church year meditations.
I. Title.
BS2565.D67   1985   242'.3   85-5125
ISBN 0-88344-244-2 (pbk.)

Published in Australia by Dove Communications, Box 316 Blackburn,
Victoria 3130
Dove ISBN 0-85924-386-9

CONTENTS

INTRODUCTION

"I came to find
what is lost."
A rather negative remark
about our lot.
　　A remark
　　not as negative
　　as it seems.
Something lost
is something lost.
It cannot be found,
but it is still there.
It is still there,
but it cannot be found.
　　To be lost
　　does not mean
　　to be completely away;
　　to be lost
　　does not mean to be destroyed;
　　to be lost
　　does not mean
　　to be forgotten.
　　　　The key
　　　　I lost in my room
　　　　is still there,
　　　　only I don't know
　　　　where.
　　　　I forgot
　　　　where I put it.

1

Once among us,
he started his search,
and the gospel
about him
is the story of him
finding
what he was looking for:
    in Mary and Joseph;
    in the shepherds and the wise men;
    in Simeon and Anne;
    in Mary, the prostitute;
    in Zaccheus, the rich swindler;
    in Nicodemus, the scribe;
    in Peter, the traitor;
    in the man who was possessed
    by a legion of evil spirits;
    in the one who was running bare
    through the naked mountains;
    in the smallest of children;
    in the greatest of sinners;
he found
—in all of them—
what he was looking for:
    the fingerprints of the hand of his Father,
    traces of divine origin,
    the perfume of God's breath,
    the Spirit our creator
    had blown,
    from the very beginning,
    in all of them,
    in all of us.
He loved to tell his stories
about lost items
which were found:
    a sheep,
    a coin,
    a treasure,
    a pearl,
    a child.

He had not only come
to find what got lost;
he added:
"I came to give life,
life to the full!"
     His work
     was not only
     a kind of restoration,
     a polishing up,
     a bringing to former splendor,
     salvation and redemption;
     he came to enhance creation,
     to bring it to fullness;
     he spoke about a harvest time.
He came to give us,
and the whole world,
the plants and the animals,
the sky, the water, and the earth,
new hope.
     A hope based
     on the life
     God
     blew into our human family,
     from the very beginning,
     saying:
     "It is good,
     it is very good."
A life
growing in us
all the time,
through misery and disaster,
through suffering and cross,
into the glory
of our risen life.
     A hope
     drawing near,
     very near.

1.

ABOUT THE END

Jeremiah 33:14–16
1 Thessalonians 3:13–4:2
Luke 21:25–28, 34–36

According to yesterday's papers
a bishop in Kenya
said in a graduation talk
at the Gaba Pastoral Institute
that the Christians
in this country
do not sufficiently think
about what he called
the *eschata*:
the ultimates,
the end.
    I do not know
    in what kind of world
    that bishop lives.
    It is definitely not the world
    in which we live,
    because in that world
    those ultimates
    —death,
    and especially the death and end
    of this world—

4

are very often thought
and spoken about.
It happens so often
that you hear people say
at this university,
"Look at what is happening
around us,"
     and they are thinking then
     about the weather,
     the sun and the moon,
     wars and starvation,
     the agony of the nations,
     atomic threats,
     and the possibility
     of the shaking of heaven itself.
They do all this
in fear,
in great fear.
They speak about those things
in terms of punishment.
They will state
that they can understand
that God wants to punish
this world and humanity
considering our sins
and iniquities.
     They even quote the Bible.
     Didn't the prophet Isaiah say:
     "The day of the Lord is coming,
     that cruel day
     of his fierce anger and fury;
     the earth will be made into
     a wilderness,
     and every sinner will be
     destroyed.
     Every star and every constellation
     will stop shining;
     the sun will be dark
     when it rises,

and the moon will give
no light."
Sometimes a very lovely person,
a beautiful secretary
with very large brown eyes,
will speak like that.
She will say:
"I can understand very well
that God is fed up.
Not a single one of God's laws
is kept.
I can understand very well
what God plans to do.
God is going to destroy us."
And she looks
as if she means
what she is saying.
Maybe she does.
Many people do.
The apostles did.
Do you remember
how they reacted that day
when they were not received
by one or another village
in Samaria?
The people in that village
had closed their gates on Jesus.
And all his followers reasoned
like that secretary
and said:
"Get the sun down,
let the moon fall on them,
shake the powers of heaven,
punish them,
burn them to cinders."
Jesus said to them:
"Can you please be quiet?
You don't understand me at all.
You aren't of my spirit."

That is what he says
in the gospel reading of today.
He speaks about the end
not in punishing terms.
He speaks about the end
not threatening with hell fire
and murder.
He speaks about the end
in a way
that the end itself
brings fulfillment,
power and glory:
the son of God
bringing to an end
all our struggles.
He will bring it all
to an end himself.
It is good to know that.
If we did not know that
we might get swamped in despair
or in a false hope
that eventually would turn
into a nightmare.
If we did not believe
that he will take over,
why should we be busy now
at all?
All our utopian thinking,
the idea that we will be able
to change it all,
would be thwarted and frustrated
again and again.
We would not be able to be sure
of a real new future.
In HIM we have
that certainty.
He will come,
he is on the way,
reaching out his hands;

and we should be on our way
to him,
reaching out our hands.
      Our position is like that man
      who fell in a river.
      Taken up by its current
      he swims as much as he can;
      he advances somewhat,
      but the current is stronger.
      He is going to lose,
      he is going to drown,
      he is going to disappear.
      Then all of a sudden
      help arrives
      from the riverbank:
      a man steps in the water,
      he stretches out his hand,
      he gets nearer and nearer,
      but the drowning man
      has to do whatever he can
      to be saved by that hand.
      They reach out to each other
      and straining their forces
      —both—
      he is saved.
That is how we are
in the current of this world.
We reach out to him,
straining ourselves
as well as we can,
and he is reaching out to us
in view of the final salvation,
the final change,
the end
and the beginning.
Amen.

2.

POINTING AT JESUS

Baruch 5:1–9
Philippians 1:4–6, 8–11
Luke 3:1–6

Before Luke introduces
John the Baptist
to us,
he depicts
a tremendous backdrop.
    He speaks about
    the fifteenth year of the reign
    of Emperor Tiberius
    in Rome,
    calling up the imperial powers,
    its armies and weapons,
    its "stability," "peace,"
    and "law";
    its "order" and its tax system,
    its conquests,
      trumpets, and banners.
He indicates
the political rulers of the time:
Pontius Pilate in Judea,
Herod in Galilee,

9

Philip in Iturea and Trachonitis,
and Lysanias in Abilene.
>He writes about the high priests
>Annas and Caiaphas,
>evoking
>the mystery of their
>religious influence,
>the temple and its sacrifices,
>its incense, prayers,
>visitors, hymns, processions,
>and innumerable
>officials.
And then, against this powerful background,
full of the leaders
of his time,
Luke suddenly speaks
about
the word of God
that came to a man who
—outside of all this—
had been living
in the desert:
JOHN.
>He had been living
>in that desert for so long
>that he was almost part of it:
>he ate its food,
>he dressed in the skins of its animals
>he smelled like it,
>he looked like it.
Once called by God
this man went,
on his own,
through the whole Jordan district
preaching repentance,
beseeching people
to change their ways,
to prepare
for the final kingdom of God.

A kingdom
that had been foreseen
by Moses
and all the other prophets,
but a kingdom
that had never been realized
as yet.
     John started that mission
     on his own,
     alone,
     just like the Word of God
     had come only
     to him.
People came to listen to him,
true.
A group formed itself around him,
true.
People talked about him,
once they were home again,
true.
He even became the topic of conversation
at Herod's court,
true.
     But essentially
     John remained alone.
     The day Jesus stood
     in the crowd before him,
     it was only John
     and nobody else
     who recognized him
     and pointed at him
     saying:
     "There is Jesus!"
     Nobody else
     had recognized him,
     nobody else
     even saw him.
     It was John,
     only John,

who pointed him out
to us.
In the second reading of today
Paul writes to
the Philippians
and to us:
that he is so glad
that the word of God
came to all of us,
and he adds
that he enjoyed hearing
that we,
all of us,
are spreading the good news,
that all of us,
like John,
point at Jesus.
Is that really true
of us?
Is that really what we do
under the influence of
the word of God
that came to all of us?
Do you *ever* point at Jesus
in this world
as John would have done?
Aren't the ones,
who are doing it
in the world in which we live,
almost as lonely
as John
in the world in which he lived?
If John would not have
pointed at Jesus
that day,
nobody would have noticed him.
If we don't point at him
now,

who will see him,
who will notice him?
If we don't point
at his influence among us,
how will he ever be known
at all?

3.

HAPPY REALISM

Zephaniah 3:14–18a
Philippians 4:4–7
Luke 3:10–18

Today the three readings
speak about happiness
and expectation.
Zephaniah says:
"Rejoice,
for the Lord *will be* with you."
Paul writes:
"Be happy,
once more I tell you
be happy,
because the Lord is *near.*"
John the Baptist preaches:
"Be prepared,
because someone *is coming*
who is going to change
all of you,
and consequently
the whole of the world."
　　All this sounds very nice,
　　its sounds very promising,

14

and yet
it resembles too much
that type of situation
we all know so very well
from our daily lives.
You need something
from someone:
        a form,
        a recommendation,
        a letter,
        a reference,
        a document,
and every time
you go to his office
or his residence
he says:
"Oh yes, of course,
no difficulty at all.
Can you please come back
tomorrow?"
        You go back "tomorrow"
        and again the answer is:
        "Oh yes, of course,
        no difficulty at all.
        Can you please come back
        tomorrow?"
        And you go back "tomorrow"
        and the answer is:
        "Oh yes, of course.
        Can you please come back
        tomorrow? . . ."
And those "tomorrows"
never ever change into
today.
        There is something else
        that is very unpleasant
        about those texts.
        They seem to suggest
        an optimism that is,

      as is most optimism,
       unrealistic.
You know what optimism is.
In a magazine published recently
the optimism
of the president of the U.S.A.
is described
and castigated.
The article says:
"You can give that President
a list of twenty consequences
of his actual policy;
nineteen of those consequences
foretell doom,
and only one out of the twenty
is hope giving.
He will forget about
the nineteen negative ones
and concentrate completely
on the one that was positive.
And he will say:
'Didn't I tell you
that things will go well?' "
      Aren't all those
      who see the kingdom of God
      growing among us
      like that?
      Aren't they attentive
      to small developments,
      to small happenings
      in the midst of the rapidly
      deteriorating situation
      of this world?
Isn't it nonsense to say
that things go well?
Isn't it ridiculous
to expect people to be happy
about a TOMORROW
that never seems to come?

The Jewish people
must have been thinking like that
while they were marching
for forty years
through the desert:
Be happy,
the day will come;
be happy,
all goes well;
but the day was delayed,
and delayed and delayed. . . .
Nevertheless, they went on marching
and every day
God showed them
his protection and assistance:
the birds that fell down
from heaven,
the manna they found
in the sand,
the water that sprung
from dry rock,
the children
born.
     It is in that way
     that we too are marching
     through a desert.
     We did not yet arrive.
     We have to march on
     and on and on. . . .
Zephaniah wrote:
"Don't let your hands
hang limp!"
Paul wrote:
"Be kind to everyone!"
John preaches:
"Convert, change."
     And all three of them
     give the same reason
     for what they recommend:

it is the Lord
who accompanies you,
    the true Lord!
It is easy to be pessimistic
in the world
in which we live;
it is easy to be optimistic
if you close your eyes.
    But let us be
    happy realists,
    counting our blessings
    and marching on
    towards life
    in the full.
    Amen.

4.

FULL OF GRACE

Micah 5:1–4a
Hebrews 10:5–10
Luke 1:39–45

The beginning had been
that angel coming to Mary.
Considering the date of Jesus' birth
on the 25th of December,
it must have been the 25th of March.
       That angel greeted her
       saying:
       "Hail Mary,
        full of grace!"
That is how it started,
full of grace.
That grace was, of course,
not some *thing*.
That grace did not fill her
like water fills a bottle,
or salt a bag,
or books a box.
       That grace
       was her being taken up
       in God's plan.

19

That grace was her mission.
That grace was what she was going
to mean
to all of us.
The angel did not only tell her
about the role she was asked
to play.
It also said:
"Listen, your old aunt,
Elizabeth,
conceived too
in her old age,
and though she is so very old,
she is already
in her sixth month."
And Mary
who had said
"Yes"
to her Lord
already,
stood up,
packed her things
—she was still free,
Joseph had not yet taken her
into his house—
and hastened
over the mountains
and through the valleys
to her aunt.
When I was a child,
I remember
that I always wondered
about the heroes
in the books I read:
the cowboys and Indians,
the supermen and superwomen
of that time.
They did marvelous things,
great things,

but they never did the things
that hold human life together
and make it possible.
    You could read
    a whole book
    without their even drinking
    one cup of coffee
    or of tea;
    they never needed
    their father or their mother;
    they never had to go to
    a wash room;
    they never brushed their teeth,
    or polished their shoes;
    they never ate breakfast;
    and so on.
And even nowadays
I am sometimes struck
if I hear about the heroes
of these days,
the good ones and the bad ones.
Do they ever live a normal life?
Do they ever do
a normal thing?
    In the case of Mary
    I never felt
    those difficulties.
    She just had been made
    into the mother
    of the whole of the human future
    but when she,
    full of grace,
    heard
    about her old aunt,
    she veered up,
    like only a girl of sixteen
    can do,
    and she ran off
    to help.

Elizabeth
was in her sixth month
and she was very old.
She was so old
that John in her womb
began to tell on her.
She was alone;
she felt shy about her condition.
Zechariah, her husband, was a dead loss
since he had come back
totally dumb
from the temple one day.
>   The waterjugs
>   she had to fill at the well
>   seemed heavier and heavier
>   everyday;
>   she had difficulties
>   in getting her things washed
>   on the rocks
>   in the river;
>   and she had sometimes
>   terrible pains in her back
>   because her old frame
>   had difficulties
>   in accommodating
>   that young, jumpy,
>   prophetic new life.
>   And there was no one
>   to massage her back
>   from time to time.
But then one day
she saw,
looking out of her window,
Mary
coming around the corner,
her bouncy, healthy,
young, and robust
cousin.

She knew
her trouble was over
and she burst out
in joy.
    Joy not only
    because she recognized
    in Mary
    the mother of her savior,
    but joy also
    because she knew
    that Mary,
    full of grace,
    would be a grace
    to her
    in her difficult days.
Mary's
extraordinary mission
translated itself
into such ordinary action.
    But isn't the ordinary
    the test
    of the reality and relevance
    of the extraordinary?
    Isn't it the ordinary
    from which we live?
    Isn't it the ordinary
    he came to save?
Let us translate
the extraordinary in our lives:
the Holy Spirit
and all that
in the ordinary grace
we should be
to each other
from day
to
day.

5.

THE CHRISTMAS STORY

Isaiah 9:1–3, 5–6
Titus 2:11–14
Luke 2:1–14

Christmas is the time
when we tell our children stories,
Christmas stories.
Even parents who normally
will not tell any stories at all
will sit down,
gather their children
around their knees,
and start a story.
    Children love stories;
    stories are essential to children.
    Children know
    what all kinds of learned people
    discovered
    after very much research and study,
    that the only way
    in which you can help a child
    with moral issues,
    and with finding its way in life,
    is through stories.

24

Children are very often lost;
they do not know what to do;
they feel threatened;
they do not know how to escape;
they do not know how to relate;
they do not know what to value;
and from old,
it has always been in stories
that confusion was cleared up,
that monsters were killed,
that threats were eliminated
and relationships and values
learned.
> But, of course,
> we have to know and tell
> the right stories,
> the helpful ones.
> And that is why,
> very, very long ago
> somewhere in West Africa,
> a very wise man,
> Ananse,
> the spiderman,
> said to himself:
> "If we only knew
> the stories God tells about us."
> And he spun a thread
> straight up in the sky
> and climbing along that thread
> he arrived one day
> in front of the throne of Nyame,
> the sky-god,
> who kept all his stories about us
> in a golden box
> next to his throne.
> When Ananse asked
> for those stories,
> he did not get them
> immediately.

He had to do
three very difficult things.
But that is not the point;
the point is
that he knew
that we need those stories
by God about us
very badly.
Tonight
we heard one of them.
How God sent
a new human start,
a prince of peace,
his only son
into our midst
—God-with-us, Emmanuel—
whose life
we are destined
to pick up.
            It is a beautiful story;
            it is a story
            full of stars and angels;
            it is a story
            about shepherds and wise men;
            it is a story
            with good kings and a bad one;
            it is a story
            about murder and escape;
            it is a story
            about goodness galore.
            And yet there is a difference
            between this story
            and all those other stories
            in which heroes
            overcame darkness and evil.
The Christmas story
is a tale
based
on reality,

on a historic person,
on facts.
> And that is why we came
> together tonight,
> not only to hear that story
> once more,
> but to celebrate it,
> as the start of a new life
> among
> and even
> within us.
> A merry Christmas to you!

6.

THE WILL OF MY FATHER

Ecclesiasticus 3:2–6, 12–14
Colossians 3:12–21
Luke 2:22–40

Strange,
when speaking about the Holy Family
today,
we are confronted with a conflict,
a conflict in the Holy Family.
>You know what had happened.
>Jesus was twelve by then.
>Not yet a man,
>no longer a child,
>a rather confusing period
>for the person in question,
>and for his parents.
When leaving Jerusalem for home,
Mary noticed
that Jesus did not walk with her,
and she thought:
"Twelve.
He considers himself to be a man;
he is walking with Joseph."

When Joseph noticed
that Jesus was not walking with him,
he thought:
"Twelve.
He is still a child;
he is walking with his mother."
     It was only in the evening
     of that first day
     on their trip home,
     that they discovered
     that he had not been walking
     with them
     at all.
They were frightened;
they said:
"How is this possible?"
Next morning they rushed back
to Jerusalem
and it was only at the end
of the third day
that they found him
in the temple.
     The text reads
     that they were "overcome"
     when they saw him.
     I don't know
     what that word "overcome"
     exactly means.
     Did they weep?
     Did they jump up?
     Were they angry?
Mary told him off,
it seems.
She said:
"How could you do a thing like that?
Didn't you know
that your father and I
were worried to death?

Did you not think of us
at all?"
>He looked at her
>with his very clear eyes
>and he answered:
>"But didn't you know
>that I had to do my Father's will?
>Didn't you know
>that I must be busy
>with my Father's affairs?"
He told Mary:
"I am quite willing
to listen to you.
I am quite willing
to think of you.
I am quite willing
to love you,
but it is my Father, God,
>to whom I have to listen,
>of whom I am thinking,
>whom I am loving
>in the very first place!"
Mary did not understand,
neither did Joseph for that matter,
but Mary kept it all
in her heart,
and she understood later,
while standing
under his cross.
>In the life of her son
>something prevailed
>over all his earthly bonds.
When we speak about the difficulties
in our families
we have very much
to talk about:
quarrels,
unfaithfulness,
disobedience,

lack of respect,
the misuse of money,
and so on.
>But do we ever meet
>in our families
>the difficulty
>they were facing that day
>in Jerusalem?
>Do we ever ask ourselves
>whether we,
>within our families,
>whether we as a family,
>are interested,
>realistically and concretely,
>in the will of the Father,
>in the kingdom of God
>here on earth?
>I wonder.
>Don't we lock ourselves up
>too much
>in our family affairs and interests
>only?
Are we sufficiently open
—as a family—
to the larger issues in the world,
to the issues of the Father:
>justice,
>peace,
>unity,
>and love?
Would not such an openness
be able to help us
to overcome together
those other more internal,
more petty
conflicts
in our families?
>Jesus went home
>with them.

He obeyed them,
the text reads.
Nevertheless,
all had changed.
They knew now
what his first allegiance
was.
From then on
he was doing the work of his Father,
in the very first place,
as he would
all the rest of his life.
And so did Mary,
and so did Joseph,
as they would do
all the rest of their lives.
It is in that way
that they taught all of us
what "holiness" in a family,
in a community,
means.

7.

PACKING UP

Isaiah 60:1-6
Ephesians 3:2-3a, 5-6
Matthew 2:1-12

It must have been dark
when those wise men
saw that star.
It is possible
to see a star in daylight,
but then you have to allow
for all kinds of gadgets.
> It was in the dark of the night
> that they saw the light;
> it was in the dark of their night
> that they saw that star
> at its rising.
Notwithstanding
all their difficulties,
notwithstanding
the unbelievable troubles
of their days,
they had sufficient
faith in God
and in humanity

to pack up immediately
to follow
that star.
    It was not the star itself
    that caused them
    to follow it.
It was not its beckoning tail
—come, come, come—
that made them follow it;
it was their faith
in the possibilities
of a new world,
of a new humanity,
that made them follow.
    It is only a few weeks ago
    that a famous German female theologian
    Dorothee Soelle,
    during an interview
    for a special Christmas feature,
    was asked:
    "What does faith
    mean to you?"
    She answered:
    "It means
    that you believe
    that the kingdom of God
    is possible.
    It means that you are confident
    that this world can be changed
    in the direction
    of that kingdom.
    It means that you are convinced
    that it is not a dream,
    an illusion,
    or a figment
    of an overexcited
    religious or ethical
    mind."

"That belief,
or that faith,"
she added,
"should be so firm
and so strong
that you are willing to work
in order
to help it grow,
that you are willing
to cooperate
in its growth,
and that you don't sit down
waiting for God
to clear the situation."
It is that kind of faith
that must have been
the moving force
when those wise men
packed their luggage
and kissed their wives and children
goodbye,
facing the unbelief
and the ridicule
of their friends,
setting off
on a journey
with a destination
known and unknown
at the same time.
      Even to us,
      so many years later,
      and notwithstanding
      our belief,
      our faith,
      and our hope,
      that destination
      remains unknown,
      and yet we know.

There are hints
where it all
will lead us to,
there are indications
and signs.
    In the second reading
    of today
    Paul
    gives such a hint
    when he writes
    about a mystery,
    a mystery
    he was given knowledge of.
    A mystery,
    a secret,
    he writes,
    unknown and hidden
    to anyone
    in generations
    past.
The mystery is
that all human beings
share in the same inheritance;
the mystery is
that we all live
under the same promise;
the mystery is
that in Jesus Christ
we are all parts
of the same being,
of the same body.
    We are one,
    we belong together,
    we are all
    created in him.
    It is towards
    the realization
    of a further awareness
    of that fact

that we should strive.
That was the reason
why those wise men
—were there only three?—
packed up
and traveled
towards
him,
and towards
themselves.

8.

THE BAPTISM OF JESUS

Isaiah 42:1-4, 6-7
Acts of the Apostles 10:34-38
Luke 3:15-16, 21-22

There was something strange
about the baptisms
given by John.
They were incomplete;
they were without much effect.
John baptized;
he believed in his baptism;
but at the same time
it was John himself
who said:
>   "I am not the one;
>   I only baptize with water.
>   Wait till a stronger one comes;
>   he will baptize you
>   with Spirit and Fire."
In a way
John himself
depreciated his baptism.
Most probably
he depreciated it also

38

because he knew
that once his newly baptized disciples
were back home
his baptism
would be quickly forgotten.
And, in fact,
we don't hear very much,
nothing at all,
about the effect of those baptisms.
It seems as if
all went on
as ever before.
John knew
that his baptism
needed a complement.
And, though in another way,
maybe,
it is rather obvious
that the baptism of many Christians
seems to need
a complement
too.
Is it not true to say
that many Christians
remain as cool
as the water
that once streamed
over their heads?
Is it not true to say
that many Christians,
that many of us,
are no different at all
from the others
around us?
When you read the gospel story
of today
very carefully,
you can see
what happened to Jesus.

He must have lined up
in front of John
together with the others.
He must have stepped in the water
as his turn came.
According to Matthew
there was a short exchange
between them,
but then
Jesus was baptized.
And nothing else
seemed to have happened
to Jesus
at that moment.
Nothing at all.
He just stepped out of the water
like all the others.
And then
Luke's report continues:
*"Now when all the people
had been baptized
and while Jesus after his own baptism
was at prayer,
heaven opened."*
The others,
all the others,
went home
after their baptism
and nothing much
seems to have happened to them.
Jesus,
Jesus remained behind,
and as he started to pray,
heaven opened,
and the Spirit came down.
Could that prayer
have been the reason
that the Spirit
came down on him?

Could our lack of prayer
be the reason
that the Spirit
never seems to come down
on us?
    Weren't his disciples
    at prayer
    when the Spirit
    descended on them
    in that upperroom in Jerusalem
    at Pentecost?
There is something else
Luke remarks
in his report
on this event.
    The spirit descended
    on Jesus
    in bodily shape
    as a dove.
    In other words
    the Spirit was visible,
    just like that Spirit
    would be visible
    in all Jesus
    said, did, and omitted to do,
    afterwards.
Brother or sister,
sisters and brothers,
the story is simple:
the man from Nazareth,
Jesus,
went to John
to be baptized.
He was baptized;
the water flowed over his head.
After that baptism
he sat down somewhere,
or maybe he knelt,
he prayed . . .

and God's spirit came over him
in the shape of a visible dove,
and a voice was heard,
a voice that did not say:
"Jesus is THE SON OF GOD,"
but that said:
"JESUS is the son of God."
What would happen
if we prayed
as he did?

9.

I HAVE A DREAM

Isaiah 62:1–5
1 Corinthians 12:4–11
John 2:1–12

Yesterday
it was 54 years ago
that Martin Luther King
was born
in the United States.
    While turning on the radio
    yesterday
    I switched on
    while he was speaking.
    Those words were taped,
    of course,
    because Martin Luther King
    was killed,
    murdered,
    shot on a balcony
    by a sniper
    from behind a chimney
    in 1969.
In the speech I heard,
his most famous one,

43

he said
to an enormously enthusiastic crowd:
"I have a dream . . .
I have a dream . . . ,
that one day. . . ."
And I am sure
that many of you
would be able to fill in
what Martin Luther King
dreamt about.
I have a dream . . .
that one day
all people will sit
at one table
eating and drinking
together,
I have a dream . . . !
    Mary had that same dream
    in the gospel story of today
    when she saw her son
    coming to that wedding feast.
    It was the same dream.
    That old and ever new, human dream.
    And when she saw her son
    arrive,
    coming to that wedding feast,
    she thought:
    "Maybe
    this is the beginning of it all;
    maybe
    it is today
    when from here,
    from this feast,
    from this house,
    from this table,
    from this kitchen,
    all will start.
    Maybe
    after today

I will no longer have to say:
'I have a dream.'
Maybe
today
all is going to change.
The final wine
is going to flow."
But her son
sat down together
with some people
Mary had never seen before,
and he took a glass,
and he started to drink
like all the others,
happy and relaxed.
        Mary thought,
        "Should I try?
        Should I provoke?
        Should I suggest?
        Should I stimulate?"
While thinking like that
she heard in the kitchen,
—that is where such news is heard
first—
"No wine!
This is the last jug.
What are we going to do?"
Too many guests,
and no money either,
no solvency.
        It was as if the sign
        had been given already:
        the old was over,
        the new should start.
        She went to him
        and said:
        "They have no wine!"
He looked at her
and said:

"Not yet,
not yet."
        But she went to the kitchen,
        and ordered:
        "Do whatever he tells you."
        That is what they did
        when after sometime
        he stood up,
        went to the kitchen
        and told them to fill
        all available pots and pans
        with water.
        They filled them
        up to the brim
        and all that water
        was changed
        into wine.
John says
this was the first of the signs
that would lead to his final work.
Mary was right;
she knew
that the final banquet
would start.
She did not know
when.
Her timing was bad.
But she knew
it would come,
the time
that the dream
would be no dream anymore.
The sign was given:
he intervened in the work
she told those others
in the kitchen
to do.
*And his disciples believed
in him.*

One of those disciples,
very many years later,
was Martin Luther King
and he again
said:
"I have a dream. . . ."
But that
was not all he had;
that
was not all he did.
He worked and sweated
filling the empty jugs
of this world
with water,
sure that once again
HE would come
to change all that water,
the bitter water of this world,
into wine,
nice, grade A,
heavenly wine,
preparing for the final banquet
to come.
Let us work like him,
in the kitchen of this world,
getting prepared
for him
who will do it.
Amen.

10.

COMING HOME

Nehemiah 8:1–4a, 5–6, 8–10
1 Corinthians 12:12–30
Luke 1:1–4, 14–21

The story is simple.
He came home
for the weekend.
They had been very surprised
and when they heard
that he had returned,
they all went to the synagogue
to listen to him.
>   He came;
>   he stood up to read;
>   they gave him the book of Isaiah.
>   He took it;
>   he rolled it down;
>   and he read aloud to them
>   all the dreams
>   of that prophet Isaiah,
>   of the days to come,
>   the days of God's kingdom,
>   the days of forgiveness,
>   the days of reconciliation,

48

all his dreams
about men and women
living harmoniously together,
swords being hammered
into ploughshares,
children playing freely
without fear,
blind ones seeing,
prisoners liberated,
a period of grace.
And he said:
"That day is starting
now."
And we,
we pray
and pray
and pray
that one day
all people may live
in justice and peace together,
that one day
all swords may be hammered into
sickles and ploughshares.
And praying like that
we fail to understand him,
Jesus Christ,
who said there in Nazareth:
"THAT TIME IS NOW;
that day did come;
you are living in that last hour;
these things are fulfilled
in your generation;
it is with you now!"
The fate of our world
depends on our believing
Jesus Christ
when he says
that the hour of the kingdom
has come.

We should no longer live
with our three-dimensional
time-concept:
the past,
the present,
and the future.
We, his followers,
the ones who take his stance
in this world,
should live his two-dimensional time:
the past,
whose evil aftereffects
have to be overcome
—that must have been the reason
that Jesus
in all his postresurrection appearances
stressed forgiveness so much—
and *the present*,
the NOW of the kingdom.

It is about ten years ago
that the Kenyan theologian John Mbiti
remarked that his people, the Akamba,
have a two-dimensional view of time:
a very long past,
and an extremely dynamic present.
"The future as we know it
in the linear concept of time
is virtually non-existent,"
he wrote.

A multitude of African philosophers,
theologians, economists,
anthropologists, and sociologists
denied what he said.
But that is not the issue here.
The issue is
that since the reappearance
of the risen Christ,
we Christians
should have that concept of time:

a very long past
and an extremely dynamic NOW.
The now in which
the year of grace is realized,
justice is done,
peace is made,
and the swords are hammered
into ploughshares
and the spears
into sickles.
>If that does not happen
>NOW,
>then we are unfaithful
>to him,
>and we are deceiving ourselves
>when we say
>that we are his followers.
If we only believe,
if we only hope
that all this
is only something of the future,
we will never realize it
at all.
>I think
>that it is not a question
>of not being able
>to believe in the now
>of the kingdom.
It is a question
of our unwillingness
to believe.
>We don't want to believe it
>because we know all too well
>that everything,
>our whole lives,
>would have to change.
We don't want that change
and that is the reason
that we pray and postpone,

postponing his kingdom
to a future day,
overlooking all Jesus' stories
that should shape our lives,
overlooking his words,
overlooking God's Word,
now:

> the treasure found,
> the fish caught,
> the seed sowed,
> the yeast in the dough,
> the pearl bought,
> the salt put in,
> the light put on,
> the banquet ready,
> the unwise maids
> late.

The time is now;
this is the last hour.
There is nothing to wait for
any more.
It was all given
long ago:

> aren't we that treasure,
> aren't we that fish,
> aren't we the seed,
> aren't we the yeast,
> aren't we the pearl,
> aren't we the salt,
> aren't we the light,
> aren't we the guests,
> aren't we the seven wise maids
> on time?

And all those who maintain
that the year of grace
did not come,
that justice cannot be done,
that peace cannot be made,

and that the swords
—the atomic but also
the older ones—
cannot be hammered
into ploughshares,
into sickles,
into food,
health,
and education,
as yet,
     are not of his mind,
     are not of his spirit,
     are not of his vision,
     are not his,
     whether they are
     popes,
     presidents,
     bishops,
     priests,
     or you,
     yourself,
     or me,
     myself.
     Amen.

11.

HIS EXTENDED FAMILY

Jeremiah 1:4–5, 17–19
1 Corinthians 12:31–13:13
Luke 4:21–30

Jesus had come home.
He had come to Nazareth.
It was there
that he read the text
we heard last Sunday,
from the prophet Isaiah.
It is then that he said:
"This text is being fulfilled today,
even as you listen."
It was then that he told them
the kingdom of God is
now.
    We start today's gospel
    with the sentence
    that ended the gospel reading
    last Sunday.
    It is one of the rare times
    that we find a text
    repeated twice
    in the same liturgical year.

It must be a key text;
it is.
If Jesus had spoken to them
in the way he did,
before he had left them,
before he had been baptized,
before he had received the Spirit,
before his miracles,
it would not have meant very much.
He just would have given
a commentary
as one was supposed to do
at such a service in the synagogue.
They just would have listened
to that commentary
with the same kind of interest
and fruitfulness
as when they had listened
to so many similar commentaries
and sermons
before:
interesting,
original,
well-put,
remarkable,
not bad.
But the person who was speaking
to them
that morning
had changed
after he had left.
They had heard
about his baptism;
they had heard about
the opening of heaven
—heaven that seemed to have been
closed
for so long by then—
above his head.

They had heard
about his healings,
about his exorcisms,
about his miracles.
>They had been annoyed
>and scandalized
>by those stories.
>Had he forgotten about them?
>Had he forgotten about his village?
>Were there no sick people in Nazareth?
>Did they not appreciate
>a good glass of wine?
>Why all those miracles
>in strange places?
>Why not in Nazareth?
But hearing those stories
they had also remembered
the almost forgotten rumors
and tales
told around his birth.
Hadn't there been stories
about angels and shepherds,
kings and stars,
about children killed
and a flight to Egypt?
>And that is why
>they
>jumped up
>with joy,
>when he told them
>that the kingdom of God
>had come
>to them.
>That he had come
>to tell them
>that it would start
>with them.
He won the approval of all,
and they were amazed

at the graciousness
of the words
that came from his lips.
    But then he continued,
    and instead of calling
    his miracles in Cana and Capernaum
    a mistake,
    instead of apologizing,
    he started to speak
    in even more general
    non-Nazareth-only
    terms.
He made it clear,
that his kingdom
was not going to be
just for them,
but for *all*.
He mentioned
Sidonians;
he mentioned
Syrians;
and they all
got enraged.
When they were thinking
about home,
they thought only
about themselves,
    their land,
    their water,
    their blood,
    their health,
    their clan.
When he spoke about home,
he thought of them,
all right,
but his HOME was not only
them,
his home
was his Father's home.

Coming home to Nazareth
to them,
he asked them to come home
with him
to his Father's place,
the place we all come from,
the whole of humanity,
that human-divine
extended family.
They were not ready
for that!
Are we
in this world,
in this continent,
in this country?
Are you?
Are we?

12.

ON RELIGIOUS EXPERIENCE

Isaiah 6:1–2a, 3–8
1 Corinthians 5:1–11
Luke 5:1–11

Did you notice
how there is a sudden
switch of name
in the gospel reading of today?
    The gospel starts
    with a man,
    a common fisherman,
    named
    Simon,
    and it ends with a man
    who at the end of the story
    is called
    Peter,
    meaning *rock*.
After that night
when Simon had been fishing
without catching anything,
Jesus ordered him
to throw out his nets
once more

59

near the shore
where hundreds of people
were milling around,
at a place
where no fish would dare to come
with all that noise going on.
        He obeyed
        and his nets filled
        with fish
                to the extent
                that he needed the help
                of others
                to get the nets
                into his boat.
        But it was not that catch
        that changed the man,
        that changed his name.
When handling his nets
now full of fish,
Simon was struck
by the reality
of God's presence,
and it was that experience
that changed him,
once and for all time to come.
Simon
became
Peter.
        His whole life changed
        because of that experience.
        It was that experience
        that made him
        a follower of Jesus Christ.
        And when afterwards
        people asked him:
        "How did it all start
        with you,
        Simon, sorry,
        Peter?"

he would tell them this story,
just as he must have told it to Luke,
who told it to us
today.
Some days ago
we had here in the chapel
a theological exchange.
We have that every month.
The topic this time was:
the mystery of God.
How do we know about God?
Many of us
know about God
because we are surrounded by others
talking about God,
    in school,
    over the radio,
    in church,
    and so on.
But how do those people
who seem to know about God,
know?
It must have started
somewhere,
in someone.
Talking about this,
almost all participants
remembered
that they themselves
had the kind of experience
Simon had
when he changed into Peter.
    A sister told
    how she walked once,
    when a young child,
    in the field,
    when she came across
    a brook.
    It was a beautiful summer day,

the sun was bright,
the sky was crystal-clear.
The water of the river
was not very deep.
>She took off her shoes
>and she stepped barefooted
>into the clear water.
>She saw the sun shine
>through the water
>on her feet
>and suddenly she knew,
>she felt
>that all is well with the world,
>that God keeps
>it all together.
There was a man
who told that once
he was sitting in a bus
from Naivasha to Nairobi.
Suddenly,
while doing the last slope
before Nairobi
the driver of the bus
lost control of its brakes.
The passengers in the bus
noticed it immediately.
They started to scream.
And then, our friend told us,
he suddenly felt very calm.
He said to himself:
"I am in the hands of God."
He felt it was true.
All the others screamed again
when the driver
shifted the bus into first gear
and it came to a halt
in a low ditch
alongside the road.
Everyone escaped unharmed.

I am sure that many of you
had such experiences.
Researchers over the last years
have been curious about them.
They have been asking
about them
all over the world.
They came to astonishing results,
even in a country
not well known
for its religiosity:
Britain.
Forty-four percent of the people interviewed
said that they were sure
of having had
a religious experience
and a further 30 percent said
that they thought
that they had at least one.
That means that over 74 percent
of the population
had a religious experience
or had religious experiences
during their lives!
>It is good to remember
>those experiences.
>It would be good to tell them
>to each other,
>to your parents,
>your children,
>your friends.
>It shows that
>there is in you,
>in all of us,
>access to religiosity,
>to divinity.
A saint who specialized
in religious experiences,
Saint Bernard of Clairvaux,

said long ago
that we should drink
from our own well,
from our own source
of spirituality
and religiosity.
       That is what Peter did
       and because of that
       he respected himself
       and was respected by others.
If we would know better
about each other's religious experiences,
we might respect each other more,
and ourselves too.
All of us are
full of God's Spirit,
full of dignity.

13.

THE TWO GROUPS

Jeremiah 17:5–8
1 Corinthians 15:12, 16–20
Luke 6:17, 20–26

How happy are you
who are poor now,
for yours is the kingdom of God.
    This text is often misunderstood.
    Sometimes it is misunderstood
    because it is read
    out of context.
    Sometimes it is misunderstood
    because one wants
    to misunderstand it
    in view of one or another
    ideological framework.
The first misunderstanding
tells the poor to be happy
because Jesus said so.
The second misunderstanding,
abusing the text ideologically,
tells that Jesus said
not to do anything against poverty
at all,

for mystical reasons,
and it adds
that the churches at the moment
are with the rich,
telling the poor to be happy,
to accept injustice
as a blessing,
not for mystical
but for pecuniary reasons.
     If you read the text carefully,
     those misunderstandings
     could easily be avoided.
     Jesus never made
     any blanket statement
     like
     happy are the poor,
     or *happy are the hungry,*
     or *happy are those who weep now*,
     or *happy are you when people hate you
     and despise you*.
     Never, never, never!
Let us have a look at the text.
He came down
from the mountain
that morning.
On that mountain
he had spent the night
in prayer,
as he often does
in the gospel of Luke
before an important decision.
At dawn he had called
his disciples,
and he had chosen twelve of them
to whom he gave the name
apostles,
which means:
the sent-out-ones,
the pioneers,

the messengers,
the heralds,
the scouts.
When coming down
    the thirteen
    meet two groups of people:
    the rest of his disciples,
    and an ever-growing large crowd
    that had come to hear him,
    and that had come
    to be healed.
That second group of people
did not come to follow him:
they came to hear him.
That second group of people
had not come to join him;
they had come to be healed.
    That second group of people
    had only come
    to leave him again
    as soon as possible,
    as soon as they
    heard him,
    as soon as they were
    healed by him.
They were very many,
many more
than he had
in the group of his followers
and disciples.
    Jesus makes a choice,
    and in front of that enormous crowd
    of observers
    and profiteers,
    he looks
    at the much smaller group
    of his disciples,
    those who had decided
    to follow his way,

at those who were his,
and looking at them,
in front of those others,
he said to them
and not those others:
        "Happy are you,
        happy are you,
        happy are you,
        happy are you,"
and speaking to them
against that large crowd of others,
he adds:
        "Alas for those,
        alas for those,
        alas for those,
        alas for those,
Happy are you
who are with me
to change the world,
to heal the blind,
to liberate prisoners,
to uplift the oppressed,
to feed the hungry,
to overcome injustice
to restore to everyone their dignity,
to introduce the year of grace,
of holiness, and integrity.
        Woe to you
        who remain reactionary
        when confronted
        with what became possible
        in me."
This morning we too
are listening to those words.
We too are in the crowd
in front of him.
To which of the two groups
do we belong?
        To those who are his disciples,

or to those who formed that crowd
of onlookers and profiteers,
waiting until the words are over,
waiting until the curiosity is satisfied,
waiting until we are healed,
to leave him
then,
disappearing
as quickly
as we can?

14.

HIS RESPECT FOR US

Deuteronomy 26:4–10
Romans 10:8–13
Luke 4:1–13

Anyone can see
what power can do
and what power does.
> In a way it's nice to see it:
> a mighty military parade
> with one man shouting
> ah—eh—march—
> and then thousands,
> and tens of thousands
> of soldiers
> all marching
> in the same way,
> left/right,
> left/right,
> left/right. . . .
> A nice sight
> but at the cost of a kind of
> military obedience
> that controls
> the minds, the wills, and the bodies
> of all those thousands.

Anyone can see
what popularity can do
and what popularity does
    when tens of thousands
    or hundreds of thousands
    of fans
    come together
    to see their idol:
    a singer,
    a performer,
    a leader,
    a pope.
    Every word the "idol" says
    makes their enthusiasm grow.
    They behave unusually,
    hysterically,
    ecstatically.
    But did all those fans
    not lose themselves
    in that enormous
    hero-worshipping
    crowd?
Anyone can see
what a miracle worker can do.
They are advertised regularly
on the walls of this town, Nairobi.
    Those people
    seem to have a grip
    over God,
    seem to pray authoritatively,
    and God seems
    to bend
    to their prayers,
    for suddenly
    the deaf hear,
    the blind see,
    and thousands,
    tens of thousands
    under the influence

of those signs
are suddenly
overcome,
taken over;
they pray
and convert.
> Marching along
> but forced.
> Singing along
> but infatuated.
> Praying along
> in a trance.

It is all very good;
it is all very fine;
it is all very inspired;
and yet
> the danger is
> that nothing happened
> at all.
> The danger is
> that the inner being
> of those marching,
> that the inner being
> of those chanting,
> that the inner being
> of those praying
> is not touched
> in the slightest.

Today we hear
in an obviously symbolic story
how Jesus was tempted
to make the people sing and shout
because of the *bread* given,
to make them pray and admire
because of the *sign* shown,
to make them march and obey
because of his *power* over them.
> But,
> in his respect for us,

and in his respect for the work
of the Spirit in us,
he refused.
Instead
he started to rely
on what one sometimes calls
the "tender forces"
in us.
Last Sunday
we heard about them:
happy are those who are poor
and willing to share;
happy are the merciful;
happy are those who weep;
happy are those who hunger
and thirst
for justice
and peace.
Let us believe in those forces
found in him.
Let us believe in those tender forces
found in us.
Let us believe in them,
because they were put in us
by him:
the power of the seed,
the power of the yeast,
the power of the salt,
the power of the light
of his kingdom.
Amen.

15.

HIS DREAM

Genesis 15:5–12, 17–18
Philippians 3:17–4:1
Luke 9:28b–36

Jesus had been at it
for about two to three years
by now.
He had shown them
his intentions
in all kinds of signs:
  he had been healing;
  he had been forgiving;
  he had been helping the poor;
  he had been making peace;
  he had been bringing people together;
  he had shown his glory,
  on and off,
  from time to time.
By this time it had become
clearer and clearer
that he was not going to make it,
that he was going to get
into serious difficulties,
that they were after him,

74

that he would be arrested,
that he would be eliminated.
     He himself must have been
     the first one to notice it;
     that is why he told them
     about his death
     before they had noticed,
     before they realized
     what was happening.
First,
they did not even believe him.
Peter said: "Never";
but once he had told them,
they too started
to see the signs
of the threat all around him.
They started to worry;
they started to doubt,
and maybe that was the reason
that he brought them
—eight days later—
to that mountaintop.
     There in the loneliness of that place
     they had a unique experience.
     They saw him change;
     they saw him starting to shine;
     they saw him discussing
     his death and passover
     with Moses and Eliah.
     They saw him
     in his full and final
     glory.
     They heard him affirmed
     by his (and their) Father.
     From that moment
     they knew
     —though they sometimes forgot—
     that the victory
     would be his.

They had been dreaming with him
about a new world,
about a healed humanity,
about salvation,
about the overcoming
of that old enemy,
Satan,
the opponent.
Now they knew
that all this was not only
a human dream,
but that it was
GOD'S DREAM
for humanity.
    They were taken on;
    they were enthusiastic;
    they wanted to stay;
    they shouted at him:
    "Keep it like that;
    let us stay;
    let us bake and glory
    in your shine;
    let us build something."
In a way he disappointed them
again.
He said:
"This glory will be ours,
it will be yours,
but only after the work
has been done,
only after
we have overcome
all the evil and suffering
in this world."
    They went down with him
    to continue his work
    in this world.
    He went on
    healing and preaching,

changing and converting,
showing the light
they had seen on Mount Tabor
here and there,
now and then,
being continuously busy
to make it shine
among us.
We should do that,
with his help,
under the guidance,
of his Spirit,
as much as we can,
healing,
redeeming,
liberating,
helping,
giving hope
and light,
knowing that
all darkness will be lit up,
all misery will be outshone,
and even death will be overcome
and we will be
with him.

16.

WHERE DOES THE GOOD COME FROM?

Exodus 3:1–8, 13–15
1 Corinthians 10:1–6, 10–12
Luke 13:1–9

It is sometimes almost weird
how gospel stories
written so long ago
fit in the world
in which we live.
> Take the gospel of today.
> There had been a riot
> in town
> and some people had been killed.
> They were building a tower
> in town
> and some stones had come loose
> and they too had killed.
> Did not all this happen
> over the last weeks
> in the town we live in?
> Who forgot about the violence
> in the beginning of August?

Who forgot how Stella Muka
was killed by stones falling
from Lilian Towers?
All this had been accompanied
by a question,
a well known question,
a question we all ask.
Why were those people killed,
and why did we, the others,
survive?
In Jerusalem the question
was still the more urgent
because the people killed
during that riot
had been dying
while doing some good,
while bringing their sacrifices
to the altar.
Why did those bad things happen
to good people?
We have a solution.
We think of having the answer
just like those
who went to Jesus
had their answer ready.
It is the answer we often give
when facing the same issue
in our lives.
I will tell you a story
to explain what I mean.
An eleven-year-old boy
was given an eye test at school.
They are giving those eye tests
at the moment
all over the country.
This eleven-year-old boy
was just near-sighted enough
to need glasses.
No one was terribly suprised;

his father was wearing glasses;
his mother was wearing glasses;
one of his sisters was wearing glasses;
so what?
     Nevertheless, the boy
     was very upset
     and he did not want to tell
     anybody
     why.
     But then one evening,
     just before he went to bed,
     the story came out.
     Two days before the test
     he had found some magazines
     on top of an overloaded dustbin
     somewhere in the street,
     Playboy or something like that.
     And though thinking it
     to be very naughty and bad
     he had been looking at the pictures
     of some naked men and women.
     And when the doctor told him
     only two days afterwards
     that he had to wear glasses,
     he had thought:
          "There you are.
          God started to punish me
          already.
          God is
          going to make me
          blind
          because of what
          I did."
It is that kind of issue
Jesus is confronted with
in the gospel of today.
And he tells them
very clearly
that they were wrong.

Those people were not killed
because of their sins.
Those people were not punished
because of their faults.
> If God acted like that,
> he added,
> all of you would have been killed,
> because all of you are sinners.
> If God acted like that
> all of us would be wearing glasses,
> or be blind.
> That is why
> he said:
> "If you don't change your ways
> all of you will perish."
And then he told them
that other story
about a fig tree
planted in a garden
and though exhausting the soil,
having a place under the sun,
absorbing oxygen,
and eating chemicals,
there were no fruits,
> for one year,
> for two years,
> for three years.
The owner came
to look for fruits,
and when he found none
he wanted to uproot the tree
and plant another one.
But the caretaker
convinced him
to have another try.
> While he told that story
> he must have been looking around
> at them,
> at us,

so dry,
so dry. . . .
Of course,
their question
was not answered:
where does evil come from?
Why do bad things happen
to good people?
It does, however,
answer another question:
Why is it that we find
so much goodness
and patience
in our world?
Where would all that good
come from
if God did not
exist?

17.

ON BEING LOST

Joshua 5:9a–10, 12
2 Corinthians 5:17–21
Luke 15:1–3, 11–32

The gospel story of today
can be read
in very many ways.
It is the story
of the younger prodigal son;
it is the story
of the father
who does not want to lose anyone;
it is the story
of the older son
who did not understand.
While hearing it,
you can identify yourself
with any of the three,
and you can do that
in all three cases
very fruitfully.
        You can identify
        with the lost son,
        saying: "Let me go home."

83

You can identify with the father
saying: "Let me be merciful."
You can identify with the older son
saying: "Let me open my heart."
There are so many possibilities,
let us take only one.
Let us consider
how the world in which we live
is full of lost sons and daughters,
full of lost men and women,
lost in the way
that young man was lost
when his money was spent,
when the women
on whom he had spent most of it
had left him in the cold,
when his friends too
had left him behind,
and when he had turned
to the state of a slave
herding pigs,
obliged to herd pigs
owned by a foreigner
who maybe did not even know
that a Jew
was not allowed to do that.
He was sitting there,
in the midst of those pigs,
hungry,
not allowed even to eat
the pig food.
He must have felt lost,
totally lost.

> There was a man
> who was very sick.
> He went to a government hospital
> where he should have been helped
> practically for free.
> But he was not helped at all,

because he did not know
anyone on the staff;
none of them belonged
to his family;
none of them belonged
to his people;
and he felt lost,
totally lost.
You are in the post office;
you are on line;
there is a very long line.
It is very hot;
and suddenly a man comes in.
He passes you;
he ignores the line;
and he shakes hands
with the man behind the counter
whom he obviously knows,
and you feel lost.

There are some refugees at the door;
there are so many
that they cannot be helped;
you simply don't have the money.
You are a Catholic priest;
you have to send them all away
with a shilling or two.
They go,
but one returns
when the others are gone
and says:
"Father, I am a Catholic, you know.
The others aren't,
but I am.
I can prove it.
Here is my baptismal certificate;
you must give me more."

And according to him,
all the others are lost,
totally lost.

We are too often
like that older son
who had written off
his younger brother
who had claimed his part
of the estate,
squandered it,
and then came back.
That older brother
had no pity.
He said: "He had his chance."
He said: "He spoiled it."
He said: "Let him go to hell."
And he closed his hands,
and he closed his arms,
and he wanted to keep
    the dress,
    the ring,
    and the calf,
for himself only.
That is how we treat others
because they speak differently,
because they dress differently,
because they eat differently,
and consequently smell differently.
That is how we are treated by others
because we speak differently,
because we dress differently,
because we eat differently,
and consequently smell differently.
    That is the reason
    that we don't feel at home,
    none of us,
    in this world
    but feel lost,
    totally lost.
We refuse
to take the attitude
of that Father
of all of us,

as we should
and are asked to.
    Let us forget
    about that younger one;
    let us forget
    about that older one;
    let us identify
    with the Father
    not wanting to lose anyone.
    And nobody
    will feel lost,
    us included!!
Last week we considered
why it is
that bad things happen
to good people.
The issue today is
why good things happen
to bad people.
Why do those good things
happen to them?
Why do they happen
to us?
The answer is
    because he is our Father.
    And we should be
    like him!

18.

ON NOT DRAWING A LINE

Isaiah 43:16–21
Philippians 3:8–14
John 8:1–11

That morning
obviously
Jesus did not agree
with the people
around him.
      They had been doing
      the simplest thing in the world.
      They had been doing
      something so simple
      that we are doing it all the time.
      They had been drawing a line,
      a very sharp divisive line
      between the good ones
      and the bad ones.
      They were good
      and that woman was bad,
      very bad,
      no longer worthy to live.
You heard the story.
She had been found early
in the morning;

she had been found in bed
with a man.
Maybe it was her husband
who found her.
He had raised the alarm.
Neighbors had come
out of their houses,
more and more of them;
they all liked a scandal like that.
They had taken her,
thrown her out of her house
and now they hustled her
to some Pharisees,
to some scribes,
the defenders of the law,
to ask them what to do.
They had been speaking
about mob justice,
about killing her;
but then one of the Pharisees
got an idea.
He thought:
"What if we confront Jesus
with this woman.
Let us ask him
what we should do."
     He did not want Jesus' advice.
     What he wanted was
     to catch Jesus.
If Jesus said:
"Yes, stone her, kill her,"
he would lose his good name
with the crowd;
he would no longer be seen
as the merciful miracle worker;
he would lose his popularity;
he would lose his appeal to the crowd.
     If he said:
     "No, do not kill her,"

he would be caught too
because then they would be able
to accuse him
of being against the law,
of being against their traditions.
He talked to the others;
they liked his idea
and so off they went
to Jesus
who was teaching
near the temple.
They arrived in front of him.
They pushed the frightened woman
in his direction.
They did it as if they did not even want
to touch her.
She was unclean, a sinner, dirt.
Jesus did not even look up at them;
he remained sitting,
drawing with his finger
some lines in the sand,
crosses, circles, triangles.
They told him:
"This woman here was caught this morning
in the act of adultery.
What should we do?
The law of Moses tells us
to stone her."
He did not answer them,
but when they persisted
he finally looked up
and even then he did not answer
their question at all.
He gave them
his question:
How could they draw that line
between themselves and her,
she a sinner,
and they no sinners at all.

How could they draw that line
between her and them?
And he told them:
    "All right;
    let the one of you
    who is without sin
    throw the first stone!"
They looked at him;
they looked at her;
they looked at the stones
they had ready in their hands;
they looked at each other;
and suddenly
it dawned upon them
what he meant.
    They had drawn a line around her;
    they had put her in a circle;
    they had declared her a sinner;
    but now they understood:
    they belonged in that circle too;
    they had been sinning too;
    and one after another,
    the eldest one first,
    dropped their stones
    and disappeared
    as quickly and silently
    as possible.
Her husband must have been there too,
otherwise how would she have been able
to go home safely that day
after all this?
But he too
dropped his stones
and left.
    Finally she was alone
    and Jesus looking at her said:
    "Is there no one to condemn you?"
    She answered:
    "No one."

And he said:
"I am not going to do that either,
go away,"
and then he added
—not only for her
but for all those others
who had left,
and who were in the same position
as she—
"*don't sin any more.*"
A simple story,
a story so simple
that it repeats itself among us
all the time.
How often do we not divide
the people around us
into the good ones
and the bad ones.
The group of the good ones
we belong to;
the group of bad ones
they belong to.
How often are people
not frustrating, boycotting,
arresting, torturing and executing
each other
because of that line
we draw between each other
in families,
in business,
in national and international affairs.
Jesus said:
    "That line is a lie;
    no one is good;
    you are all sinners;
    you all have to leave your ways;
    and sin no more."
    Amen.

19.

THE OPPONENT

Isaiah 50:4–7
Philippians 2:6–11
Luke 22:14–23:56

The loneliness around him
grew.
It would grow up to the point
that he was practically
alone.
It would grow up to the point
that he shouted:
"My God, my God,
why did you forsake me."
    The story begins with the twelve.
    Judas disappears;
    the three in the garden
    continuously fall asleep.
    Peter betrays him.
While that inner circle broke up,
the outer circle
disintegrated completely.
The priests
together in the Sanhedrin
declare him a blasphemer.

93

Pilate gets lost
in his cowardice
and does not know what to do.
Herod tries to play
one of his dirty tricks
on him.
And even the people,
so often the only strength
and spirit left
in days of confusion,
prefer Barabbas,
the murderer,
to him.
> When the women come to him
> on his way to the cross,
> he tells them
> that they are wrong
> and weep for the wrong
> cause.
> And finally
> once on the cross
> and bleeding to death
> alone,
> there is that one criminal
> who confesses
> that Jesus is without guilt,
> and he asks for his help.
> One,
> one who believed,
> in the last minute,
> in that very last minute,
> after he had gone
> through so much.
Notwithstanding all this,
Luke,
in his report on the Passion,
seems to take care
not to blame
anyone in particular.

In a way
the death of Jesus
seems to be due
to the circumstances
surrounding his case.

>No one is the guilty one:
>Peter turns into tears
>immediately after his denial
>because Jesus
>looks at him;
>the Sanhedrin
>takes a collective kind of
>mob decision.
>Luke never tells
>that the disciples ran away
>like the other gospel authors do.
>Luke stresses
>how Pilate tried to save him
>very sincerely
>up to the last moment.
>But he knows that one cannot do
>anything against a crowd
>that lost its head,
>and that asks
>against its own good judgment
>to free someone
>they hated:
>Barabbas.

Yet
Luke blames one:
the one called "THE OPPONENT,"
the hater,
the adversary,
the opposing spirit,
the spirit of life-denial,
the power of darkness,
SATAN.

>It was *Satan* who entered
>into Judas (Lk. 22:3);

it was *Satan* who sifted
the disciples,
and who desired
to "have" them (Lk. 22:31);
it was *Satan*
who influenced the Sanhedrin;
"Your power is the power
of darkness" (Lk. 22:53).
It was *Satan*
the enemy of life,
of human life,
using human frailty,
    human cowardice,
    human jealousy,
    human sacrifice,
    and so on,
to kill
the human possibilities,
the fullness of life
offered in
Jesus,
that man from Nazareth,
the Christ.
    We might discuss
    whether that power of evil
    should be personalized.
    Its existence among us
    seems to be beyond
    any discussion.
    That this power becomes,
    or can become,
    personalized in us
    seems to be beyond
    any doubt.
It is Luke
who warns us;
let us heed
his warning.

20.

OUR DIGNITY

Acts of the Apostles 10:34, 37–43
1 Corinthians 5:7–8
John 20:1–9

Easter is not a Sunday
on which to have a very long
sermon.
On a day like this
a sermon should be short.
The celebration of Easter
itself
is dense
enough.
    You know
    what we celebrate.
    We celebrate
    that the tomb was empty,
    some will say.
But, of course,
it is not that emptiness
we celebrate.
We celebrate
that the contents of that tomb
—now not a tomb anymore—

Jesus Christ
is risen.
    We are accustomed
    to relating that fact
    to our lives.
    He rose from the dead;
    we look forward
    to our resurrection
    from the dead.
    But, I think
    that we should relate
    the resurrection
    also in another way
    to ourselves
    and
    to each other.
So very many issues
in our lives,
in fact the issues
that make our lives
worthwhile,
    our rights,
    freedom,
    responsibility,
    love,
depend ultimately
on our belief
in the resurrection.
    There are people
    who believe
    in the absoluteness
    of our human dignity
    but who say
    that they do not believe
    in the resurrection,
    in life after death,
    but if you say so
    aren't you contradicting
    yourself?

Don't we eat plants
without any remorse
or guilt feeling
because we think them
to be momentary?
Don't many of us eat animals,
cows, pigs, ducks, and chickens,
without any hesitation
and without any qualms
of conscience
because we think them to be
temporary passengers
on the train of life?
It is on the ground
of our belief
in the resurrection
of Jesus
as a person,
and of ourselves
as persons,
that our human dignity
in its absoluteness,
in its inviolability,
rests.

It is not so long ago
that I went to visit a student
in prison.
Such a visit is not very encouraging.
You hardly can see the person
you visit
because of the layers of mesh
between him and you.
I tried to encourage him
but he said:
"Father, I am all right,
you know.
I believe in the resurrection.
Nothing can really happen
to me!"

It is that belief
in the resurrection
of each one of us
that we should live
in our daily lives,
in the way we relate
to each other.
It is the belief
that we ourselves
and the ones
we meet
will never get lost.
Alleluia.
Amen.

21.

POWER GOING OUT

Acts of the Apostles 5:12–16
Revelation 1:9–13, 17–19
John 20:19–31

The power that went out from Peter
must have been terrific;
when his shadow touched a sick person
that person was healed.
　　That power had,
　　of course,
　　something,
　　everything to do
　　with what Jesus
　　had done to him
　　that first evening
　　of that first Easter day.
　　He had told Peter
　　and all the disciples present:
　　　　"As my Father sent me,
　　　　so am I sending you!"
　　　　and he had breathed over them,
　　　　giving them
　　　　—almost like at pentecost—
　　　　God's Spirit and Life.

101

When we hear those stories
about those sick people
lined up alongside the streets
where Peter used to pass,
we accept them.
We accept them
without question.
The only ones
who sometimes ask questions
are children.
They will say:
"But why don't those things
happen anymore?"
  And maybe,
  if you are lucky,
  the child in us,
  the child in you and me,
  might ask that same question:
  "Why don't those things
  happen anymore?"
The answer is:
they do happen,
maybe on another scale,
but they do happen,
though you might not remember
or even recognize them.
  I was at a family celebration.
  Some children had been baptized.
  A lot of children were running around
  with, of course,
  the now and then unavoidable
  collisions.
  One child was hurt;
  he was hurt rather badly,
  but not too badly.
He ran to his mother
who sat him in her lap;
she put her face
against the child's face

and the pain was over
in a few seconds.
  Another child went to her father
  complaining about a headache.
  The father put one of his hands
  against the forehead of the child
  and the other hand
  against the back of her head
  and after a minute or so
  the pain was over.
I went to a hospital
some days ago.
He was very sick,
a swelling in his throat,
not too nice at all.
He was also very restless
and she sat down next to him
and took his hand,
putting her other hand
on his forehead
and he got very quiet
and peaceful.
  In all those cases
  there must have been
  something like an outgoing power,
  something like an outgoing love
  or life,
  or I don't know what.
  Where there is life,
  that life can be dynamic;
  where there is life,
  life can flow out
  and influence.
    You could say that even
    of the lower forms of life.
    Take those roses there
    on the altar.
    Aren't they unfolding
    to us?

Aren't they outgoing
to us,
with their shape, their beauty,
their color, and their perfume?
Don't they influence us?
Don't they cheer us up?
They do,
and that is why we use them
as presents to each other.
Those disciples
received his life;
we as disciples
received his life,
but that life
is so very often
locked up in us,
almost static,
as something
that is *ours* only:
MY life,
MY spiritual life.
That is why we can't give;
that is why we can't receive;
that is why we don't believe;
that is why others don't believe;
that is why we are cool
and formal and legalistic
and merely rational,
though we call all this
enlightenment.
Let us try
to live his life,
dynamically,
outgoingly,
receivingly.
Let us be plugged into
the spirit,
so that we start to shine
and to radiate,

and God only knows
what God can do through us
once we live like that.
      Let us experiment
      with the truth;
      let us experiment
      with the life
      in us
      by healing
      —but that is only one aspect—
      by counseling,
      by loving,
      by changing the world,
      by praying,
      by forgiving,
      by peace making,
      by teaching,
      by all and everything.
Once we do that,
we will discover
that all those gifts
are divided among us,
and that together
we can do
everything!
      What is your gift,
      O brother;
      what is your gift,
      O sister?
      I really would like
      to know.
      Amen.

22.

AND THEY LIVED HAPPILY TOGETHER EVER AFTER

Acts of the Apostles 5:27b–32, 40b–41
Revelation 5:11–14
John 21:1–19

In our first prayer today
we prayed:
"God, our father,
you restored the joy of our youth."
I would like to reflect with you
upon one of those joys.
There were very many of them,
but one of the joys
I remember best
is the one of listening to fairy tales,
listening to those tales
that ended with:
and they lived happily together
ever after.
    You too must still remember
    those stories
    in which terribly evil monsters,

106

dragons with shiny green eyes
and a red tongue,
spitting fire and sulphur
and living on small children,
were killed by a hero.
Stories in which witches
riding on brooms
through the night
with awful groans and shrieks
were looking for victims
to eat alive,
and who were undone
by the cleverness of a child.
Stories in which a beautiful girl
overcomes the jealousy
of her evil foster-sisters
and marries a prince in the end.
    And almost all those stories
    in which evil and disaster
    were successfully overcome
    ended with that small phrase:
    and they lived happily together
    ever after.
We might not think very much
of that end.
We might consider it
as something traditional
without any further meaning.
But, of course, it has a meaning.
It indicates that the two,
the prince and the princess,
who overcame all difficulties,
are now together.
And together
they will be able to overcome
any further difficulties
in their life
because of that bond.

That ending does not promise
that there will be no difficulties
anymore.
It does say
that in the future all obstacles
will be overcome,
because the two are now together.
It is the bond of love
between them
that will assist them
in everything.
Let us now have a look
at the gospel reading of today.
It is the final story
in the gospel of Saint John.
It is his final story
about Jesus,
about Jesus and his disciples,
about Jesus and Peter,
that same Peter
who had betrayed him so very badly
while Jesus was struggling
with all the evil forces,
the dragons and the monsters
in this world,
while he was standing
before his judges,
while he was hanging on the cross.
First Jesus invites the disciples to a meal,
to a breakfast
of bread and fish
he had prepared for them.
After that meal
—at the start of a new day—
he asks Peter,
like the prince in the fairytale
asks the princess
at the end of the story,
"Peter, do you love me?"

and Peter says: "Yes."
He asks Peter again:
"Peter, do you love me?"
and Peter answers: "Yes."
He asks Peter yet again:
"Peter, do you love me?"
and Peter says:
"Lord, you know that I love you!"
>   And then in his own way
>   at the end of the story
>   John says what all those fairy tales said:
>   *and they lived happily together*
>   *ever after.*

He does not say it like that.
It is Jesus who tells Peter:
"Very much will come your way,
many things
you won't like at all,
death on the cross included,
but really nothing will happen
to you,
because we will be together
for ever and ever.
You love me,
I love you,
follow me."
>   That was not only said
>   of Peter;
>   it was also said
>   of his other disciples.
>   It was also said
>   of us.
>   If we remain with him,
>   after all the obstacles
>   he overcame to be with us,
>   we will
>   never, never, never
>   get lost
>   ever.

We will live happily together
ever after.
But all this sounds
rather abstract,
hanging in the air,
and that is why
to end this sermon
I will tell you an almost
unbelievable story
of someone who takes
the story about Jesus
very seriously.
It happened only some days ago.
There is a small boy
hardly three years old,
Timothy,
whom I visited in a hospital.
He has been operated on
three times.
He is in pain
and one cannot drug the pain away
completely
because he is so small.
And that small boy
asked for a cross.
"A small one," he said,
"it must be small,"
most probably because
he is so small himself.
"And," said he, "Jesus must be
on it."
He got his small cross;
he looked at it;
he asked to put it in a place
where he could see it
when in pain,
all the time.
That small boy Timothy
understood
the end of our story of Jesus,

how pain was overcome,
and they too will live happily together
ever after.
Amen.

23.

WHAT GOOD IS THIS SHEPHERD?

Acts of the Apostles 13:14, 43–52
Revelation 7:9, 14–17
John 10:27–30

Some days ago
we had a funeral
in this chapel.
A funeral of a small child,
hardly two years old.
>He had been baptized
>some weeks ago
>in Kenyatta National Hospital's
>intensive care unit.
>While he was being baptized,
>Joseph
>—that was the name he got—
>was connected
>by all kinds of tubes and pipes
>to machines
>that helped him survive.
>He stayed in that hospital
>for more
>than four weeks,

struggling against death,
but then one morning
at 11 A.M.
he gave up.
There were very many people
in the chapel.
The family was,
of course,
very sad.
Because of some delay
at the city mortuary
the cortege
arrived late
and people were waiting outside
in front of the chapel.
You could easily overhear
their conversations.
So many asked
that famous question
always asked at such an occasion,
a question
that is asked
almost from bed to bed
in any Nairobi Hospital:
"Why did this happen?"
"Why did God not intervene?"
"Why was this life ended
so prematurely?"
"Does God bother at all?"
"Does God really exist?"
A difficult question.
A difficult question
especially if you read it
against the background
of the gospel of today.
The gospel in which Jesus says:
"I am the good shepherd.
The sheep that belong to me
listen to my voice.

I know them
and they follow me.
I give them eternal life.
They will never get lost.
No one will ever steal them from me!"
    That text calls up
    an idyllic, an Arcadian, a rural scene
    with peacefully bleating sheep,
    accompanied by their playful young
    in a very rich meadow
    with lush, green grass,
    with flowers and butterflies,
    chirping birds and insects,
    a blue sky,
    a nice sun,
    and an elderly, pleasant shepherd
    full of care for his sheep,
    within his bag
    everything that might be needed
    when something goes amiss.
The Lord is my shepherd,
there is nothing I shall want.
    Is that really true?
    Was Joseph not baptized?
    Were his parents not baptized?
    Weren't they God's sheep?
    What good is that shepherd?
But then
there is that second reading
from John today,
a reading from the book of Revelation,
a reading from the Apocalypse,
the last book of the Bible
and, therefore,
maybe a commentary
on all the other books.
    In that reading too,
    Jesus is said to be their shepherd
    who will take care
    that they will never thirst again,

that the sun and the wind
will never plague
them any more,
that their tears will be wiped away.
That text implies very clearly
that before then
those sheep,
those people
went through all kinds of trouble.
They were thirsty;
they were burnt by the sun;
they dried up in the wind;
they were plagued;
they wept;
they went through the enormous
persecution
that soiled their clothing;
they got wounded
and very dirty.
Two periods are indicated
by John:
—one of struggle and difficulties
—one of bliss and peace.
It is rather obvious
that we are living
in the first period,
a period of thirst,
thirsting for justice;
a period of struggle,
struggling for peace;
a period in which we are soiled,
wounded, plagued, grieved
and often in distress.
At the same time
we seem to live already
in that second period
where it is *he*
who leads us
in our lives,
who keeps us together,

    makes us care for each other
    when we listen to his voice.
During the funeral of Joseph
a member of his family
gave a eulogy.
In that eulogy
for that child of two
we were told
how much Joseph had meant
to his parents,
his two sisters,
and his brother.
The eulogist spoke
about the struggle of the boy
with death,
but also about his parents
who helped him
as much as they could.
He spoke about the pain,
and the evil, and the fever,
but he also was thankful
for the care and love
shown by the doctors
and the nurses
of the hospital.
He spoke about the sorrow of the parents,
but he also expressed his gratefulness
to all the friends and family members
for their attention,
their comfort,
the sympathy,
and their consolation.
    Good and bad.
    In all that badness and sadness
    there was so much good,
    so much listening
    by so many
    to the voice of God,
    to the voice of the Good Shepherd!

And it is
in that way
that all of us
are led
through this valley of death
to the kingdom to come.
Amen.

24.

AN ENDING TASK

Acts of the Apostles 14:21-27
Revelation 21:1-5
John 13:31-35

Two readings today,
the two last ones,
are about an end.
     In the book of Revelation
     John writes about the end
     of the old earth
     and the old heaven,
     and in the gospel
     John writes:
     "When Judas had gone . . . ,"
     another end
     to an affair.
When we hear about that first end,
the end of this world,
very many among us
become afraid.
I am sure that very many among us
have already counted
how old they will be
in the year 2000

118

because they fear
that in that year,
with its magical number 2000,
the world might end.
    That is what
    very long ago
    Christians also thought
    when the year 1000
    was approaching.
    You can read
    in the history of architecture
    how people stopped
    designing and building
    churches and big buildings
    because they thought
    the end was near.
    And you can also read
    how, once that year was over,
    all over Christendom
    the building started
    again.
Some among us
are not only afraid.
They point at the earthquakes,
the disasters, the famines,
the signs in heaven,
the build-up of our atomic weapons
and all kinds of things like that
and say:
"Watch out,
the end is near."
It is as if we don't like ends,
and very often we don't like ends,
but sometimes we do.
Think about work,
any work,
any real work you do.
Let me illustrate
what I mean.

Just imagine
that someone organized
a song festival,
and during that song festival
no song was sung.
Or think of a philosophers' congress,
an international one,
but during that congress
those philosophers
did all kinds of things,
sail, deep sea dive,
garden, cut grass,
paint, sculpt,
fish, keep bees or birds,
or I don't know what,
but they never
philosophized.
Think about a swimming contest,
where not only does no one swim,
but no one even goes
to a swimming pool.
Rather obviously all this
would seem very strange.
Singers should sing
when celebrating their singing;
philosophers should philosophize
when celebrating philosophy;
swimmers should swim
when celebrating
humanity's ability
to move through water.
But on Labor Day
when we celebrate our
human work
we do that
in a very strange way:
by very carefully doing no work at all
for the whole day.
Strange,
very strange indeed,

but showing
our very ambiguous attitude
to work.
        Do you know
        that very old myth
        about a man call Sisiphys?
He was a man
punished by the gods;
I forgot why.
His punishment consisted in work.
He had to roll a big rock
to the top of a mountain.
It took him the whole day
to get that rock to the top,
a whole day of heavy work,
but when he was almost at the top,
just a few yards from it,
the slope of the mountain
was so steep
that the stone slipped away
and he had to start all over again.
And each day,
day after day,
the same thing happened.
Those gods had constructed
that mountain in such a way
that it had to happen.
And he would be dismissed
and sent home
to his wife and children
only when that stone was set
on the top of that mountain.
        Sisiphys suffered
        terribly
        because he worked in vain,
        and he knew it.
        Sisiphys suffered
        terribly
        because he knew
        there was no end to his task.

Just imagine
that there would be no end
to the task Christ gave us
in this world.
Just imagine
that there would be no end
to this world
and to our struggle
in this world
for health and peace,
for justice and harmony.
> It would be terrible
> and that is why it is good
> to read today
> in the book of Revelation,
> that one day
> this world will be over,
> that one day
> our work will be done,
> that one day
> the last tear will be wept
> and glory and fulfillment
> will start.
The gospel reading
explains
how this will happen:
when Judas had gone,
when the one
who stood as a symbol
for all evil in the world
had left,
that night,
Jesus said,
rearranging his dress
and calling their attention:
"*Now*
my glory
and your glory
can start."

It will start
when evil is
overcome.
In English the word "labor"
means work.
It has also another meaning.
It can mean
the trouble
a woman has
when giving birth
to a baby,
to new life.
  That is how
  we should see
  our labor
  in our lives,
  in our families,
  in our world:
      giving birth,
      giving new life
      to a new world
      and a new heaven,
      together with HIM.
      Amen.

25.

JERUSALEM

Acts of the Apostles 15:1–2, 22–29
Revelation 21:10–14, 22–23
John 14:23–29

Some days ago
I was called to a family.
Something very sad
had happened
to that family.
One of their grandmothers
was visiting them.
During the night
she must not have felt well
and she had gone to the sitting room
to eat or to drink something.
There she was found
early in the morning
by one of her grandchildren.
She was dead.
  Nobody knew what to say;
  nobody even knew what to think.
  But then her daughter said:
  "I am sure,
  she is now up there!"

and she pointed at heaven.
But then someone else said,
I think it was the granddaughter:
"No. I think
she is down here,
with us."
>   Strange, where do we go?
>   Where is heaven?
>   Where is the new Jerusalem?
>   Where did Jesus go?
I read a story yesterday evening.
It was not really a story.
It was a report
on somebody
who was in a hospital.
I will read it to you:
>   "In December Cochan fell ill
>   with congestive heart failure.
>   I went to the hospital to visit her
>   in the intensive care unit.
>   I found her sleeping
>   and did not want to disturb her,
>   so I sat and waited.
>   Within a few minutes
>   her eyes opened wide
>   and a broad smile
>   bloomed across her weather-beaten,
>   freckled face.
>   It was a moment I shall never forget.
>   Unable to speak,
>   she began to spell out a word
>   on the bedsheets.
>   With labored movements
>   her finger finally spelled out
>   the word
>   home: *home.*
>   On January 4th,
>   late in the afternoon
>   Cochan went quietly
>   home."

I don't know
if you saw the film *ET.*
It is playing at the moment here in town.
I'm not telling you to go there,
but I went there.
I was curious
to see a film
that seems to be
the greatest money-maker
of all times.
It has attracted, it seems,
more visitors
than any other film ever made.
Why?
Why do people go to see it?
Why is it so attractive?
It is about ET,
an *extra-terrestrial* being
from another planet,
from outerspace.
It is a very
friendly being
with a nicely glowing heart.
In that glow
withered plants start to bloom,
aggressive animals become peaceful,
and a fighting family
turns into a nicely caring one.
> The being cannot communicate
> in human language,
> but being very intelligent
> it quickly picks up some words.
> And the first word it picks up
> is *home*;
> home,
> I want to go home.
The whole rest of the film
is only on how it gets
home.

Why do so many of us,
millions and millions,
go to see that film?
Is it because we too
don't feel at home here
and would like to go home,
to where we came from?
In the gospel of today
Jesus speaks about
his going home.
He even
tells us
that we should be glad
to hear
that he is going home
to his Father.

Yet, even in his case,
that whole home-issue
seems to be
very confusing
and very strange.
He says:
"I am going home
to my Father,"
and then he adds:
"If anyone of you loves me,
he will keep my word,
my Father will love him,
and we shall come to him
and make our home
with him."

Where is that home?
Where is our home?
Where is Jesus?
Where is heaven?
Where is the Father?
Out there?
Up there?
Or here?

It is John
who in the second reading of today
gives an answer.
He wrote:
"In the spirit,
the angel took me to the top
of an enormously high mountain
and showed me Jerusalem,
the Holy City,
coming down from God
out of heaven."
    When John
    was
    told to look
    at the new earth,
    when John was told
    to look
    at the new heaven,
    when John was told
    to look
    at Jerusalem,
    he had to look down!
    He had to look
    to the world;
    it was there that things
    had been happening.
    It is here that things happened.
    It is here that God is with
    his people.
    It is here that they are
    together with him.
John saw that new world,
that new heaven,
Jerusalem,
in its fulfillment.
It was a vision.
We are not yet so far;
we are still living
under the promise

of those first words
in the gospel:
"If anyones loves me
he will keep my word,
and my Father will love him
and we shall come to him
and make our *home*
with him."
     To love him
     does not only mean
     to be kind-hearted to others
     and not to wish them any evil.
     To love him
     does not only mean
     to be on friendly
     terms with our Lord
     in prayer or something like that.
     To love him means to keep his word,
     and that word is the realization
     among us
     of that new Jerusalem,
     together with each other,
     together with him
     until one day
     all will be good
     again,
     as it was in the beginning
     and ever will be.
     Amen.

26.

IN AND OUT

Acts of the Apostles 1:1–11
Ephesians 1:17–23
Luke 24:46–53

Jesus,
who had been living
for thirty years with them,
went up to heaven.
　　The same Jesus
　　had always been telling them
　　that he felt so much a part
　　of the human family
　　that he should be considered
　　as one of us.
　　He had compared us together with him
　　with a plant;
　　he had compared us together with him
　　with a body:
　　he being the trunk,
　　we being the branches;
　　he being the head,
　　we being the body.
　　　　When that head,
　　　　this one of us,

130

entered heaven,
all of us
made it too.
Did this ever happen to you?
There is a man at the door,
not necessarily a beggar;
he could be a salesman,
a hawker,
or anyone else.
    He wants to come in,
    but you don't trust him
    so you try to close the door in his face,
    but you don't succeed
    because he put his foot,
    with a sturdy, thick-soled boot,
    in the door,
    and however hard you try to push,
    you can't close that door
    again.
    You are caught.
I don't think
that such a person
would ever try to push his head
through the crack of that door.
It would be too dangerous for him,
and for you too
because if his head would be in,
he himself is in:
wherever your head can pass,
you can pass too.
    That is why people
    who put grills and bars on their windows
    to keep others out,
    and themselves in,
    never leave openings
    big enough
    to let a head through,
    because if the head of a normally built person
    is through,

all the rest can easily follow,
   so they say.
This has been true
for all the time of our existence.
If we were born in the normal way,
everyone around the mother we were born from
knew
that once our head was through,
we would be through.
      If our head
      is in heaven already
      we must be there
      in a sense
      too.
That is what he said
before he went.
He did not only say
you are going to come
where I am now.
He said that too.
He told them
that he was going to prepare
them a place.
He told them also
that he was going to send them
the Spirit from on high,
down into us
still here on earth,
not yet born
into the heavenly light,
and with that power
in us
we should realize heaven around us
here in this world.
I am sure
that you know of instances
when that happens
now and then.

It should happen
more and more
because we are already in,
though still out.

27.

BREAKING LOOSE

Acts of the Apostles 2:1–11
1 Corinthians 12:3–7, 12–13
John 20:19–23

Afraid
of the people in the street,
they locked themselves in,
no communication,
doors closed,
windows shuttered,
curtains drawn,
a piece of paper
in the opening of their hearth.
 We might think
 that this was
 because they had not received
 the Holy Spirit.
 But according to the readings today,
 they had received the Spirit already
 fifty days before.
 The gospel tells
 that on the evening of the first day of the week
 —after his death and resurrection—
 Jesus had come

and he had given them
the Holy Spirit,
breathing over them
the breath of the new creation,
just like his father had done
so many millions of years before
over those first human beings,
Adam and Eve.
The Spirit was there;
the Spirit did not work;
it did not live
because they were afraid.
They were afraid
of the people in the street;
they were afraid
of the world around them;
they were afraid of themselves,
full of that Spirit.
What we are celebrating today
is, therefore,
not the coming of the Holy Spirit in them.
We are celebrating
how on that fiftieth day,
Pentecost,
that Spirit in them
could no longer be contained
within the limits of their fear,
how the spirit suddenly,
in thunder and lightning,
in multiple flames,
burst loose
in their hearts
and above their heads.
It was a fire
that did not come from outside them
alone;
it was a fire
that came from within them
too.

It was a fire
that made them
finally move.
>We are not different from them;
>they were not different from us.
>We too received the Spirit
>ages ago,
>even more that fifty days ago,
>but in us too,
>no communication,
>doors closed,
>windows shuttered,
>curtains drawn,
>all exits covered
>with pieces of paper.
>We, too, are afraid
>of the people in the street,
>of the world around,
>of the Spirit in us.

That Spirit is safely
hidden;
it is nicely
kept;
it does not move us
at all;
and in silence we say:
"Thanks be to God."
>We know
>that if the Spirit broke loose
>in us,
>we would have to change,
>all would change,
>and that is why
>we have conditioned that Spirit
>carefully
>in us:
>>by letters and laws,
>>by regulations and rules,
>>by traditions and institutions.

We gave that Spirit
a permanent home,
we thought,
locked in
without taking any risks:
no experiments,
no overtaxing of our possibilities,
no exaggerations, please,
duly measured only.
    That is what they thought,
    that is what they hoped,
    but suddenly they could not contain
    God's power anymore.
    It burst loose in them,
    and before they knew
    what had happened to them
    they were standing in the street,
    they were standing in the world
    they had been afraid of
    before.

28.

SUMMING UP

Proverbs 8:22–31
Romans 5:1–5
John 16:12–15

Trinity Sunday
is the last Sunday feast of the year.
There are still many Sundays to come,
twenty-five to be exact,
but they all will simply be Sundays of the year,
Sundays after Pentecost,
Sundays about what the Spirit
should do in our lives.
　　This is the last feast,
　　and as so often happens
　　after the end of a period
　　before starting a new season,
　　we are invited this Sunday
　　to sit down,
　　to close our eyes,
　　to ban all noise,
　　and to reflect upon
　　what happened to us.
　　We are asked to make an accounting,
　　to sum up.

So let us sit down,
let us close our eyes,
let us ban all noise,
let us reflect upon
what happened to us,
making accounts and summing up.
> That summing up
> is happening more often
> than we might think.
> If you are aware
> of what is happening around you,
> you will understand what I mean.
How often does this not happen?
There is that woman who tells you
the disaster of her marriage:
everything went wrong
from the very beginning.
She finally gave up;
she left her husband;
she took the children with her;
and then
when it all has been told
she will say
while *summing up:*
"Yet, I know that God cares.
God will help me.
God helped me before.
I know,
I know."
> There is that man
> who is very happy;
> all went very well;
> he is happy about everything;
> he is successful in business;
> he has a splendid career,
> and good health;
> and he too speaks to you,
> and *summing up* he says:
> "I am so grateful.

I am so blessed.
I know that God provides.
God is my shepherd.
I know,
I know.''
There is that refugee
who says:
''I know it is a temptation;
I should not even think about it;
but nevertheless
I would like to finish;
I would like to end my life,
but God will not forsake me.
God is with me.
God is with us.
God will help me.
I know,
I know.''

Did you listen to the prayer
we just prayed?
It is the prayer of this Sunday.
It reads:
''You reveal yourself
in the depths of our being.''
According to that prayer,
God is in us,
in our consciousness
from within.
Do you remember how we thought
last Sunday,
on Pentecost,
that the little flames
might have come from outside,
but that they also might have come
from within,
as they received the Spirit?
Listening to that woman
summing up,
listening to that man
summing up,

listening to that refugee
summing up,
> to them it all came
> from within.
It was
while they were expressing themselves to us
that they knew
about those depths
in their hearts.
Listening to them,
we knew too,
we felt too,
in the depths of our hearts:
> There is a God who cares
> as a father and mother;
> there is a God next to me,
> as a brother, a companion, a friend,
> any brother, any companion, any friend,
> but especially Jesus.
> There is a Spirit with me.
> There must be
> because I know all this
> *from within!*
Today,
brothers and sisters,
we are here
to tell each other
about that belief in a Father,
a Brother,
and a Spirit,
full of hope,
notwithstanding all rumors and disasters,
and thanks to all the goodness we experienced,
ready to forgive
and to share,
making us one,
their family,
from within the depths
of our being.

29.

HIS PRESENCE AMONG US

Genesis 14:18–20
1 Corinthians 11:23–26
Luke 9:11–17

Corpus Christi
is a feast
that should not be celebrated
on a Sunday.
It is a weekday feast.
It is a feast for a Thursday;
it was on that day
that Jesus had his last supper
with his followers.
  In a literal translation
  Corpus Christi means
  the body of Christ;
  a bit more freely translated
  it stands for the body and blood of Christ.
  It is for Catholics
  the feast of the blessed Eucharist;
  it is their feast of the Mass;
  it is the feast of Jesus' presence
  among us
  under the forms of bread and wine.

It is a feast
that can easily be misunderstood.
And it is often misunderstood.
The emphasis is often misplaced,
and as it is the center of our Christian lives,
and so ostentatiously the center
of Catholic practice
—practicing Catholics are the ones
who go to Mass on Sundays,
aren't they?—
misunderstanding it means
misunderstanding everything.
     Let us try
     to understand it well.
John's gospel is,
according to very many,
the most mystical of the gospels,
the most visionary one.
It was the best thought-out gospel
and the last one written,
indicating how a group of faithful,
almost a century after the birth of Jesus,
experienced him.
     John himself is described
     as a very great friend of Jesus,
     the beloved disciple,
     the youngest one too,
     the one who at the last supper
     rested with his head
     against Jesus' chest,
     the one who heard Jesus' heart
     beat.
For all those reasons,
and for any single one of those reasons,
it is very strange
that John,
when describing the last supper,
does not speak a word
about what the other gospels,

the ones of Mark, Luke, and Matthew,
mention as the main event
during that last meal he had
with them.

John gives a long series of talks,
very lofty ones,
very high ones,
and John also indicates
one thing,
one activity,
the others do not speak about.

Before the meal,
or maybe the meal had started already,
Jesus suddenly rose;
he left the table;
he went to a corner of the room;
he took off his tunic;
to the astonishment of all
he took a towel
and put it over his undergarment;
he took a pitcher full of water
and a bowl,
and he knelt in front of each of them
and started to wash their feet,
one by one.
They protested;
they did not know what they were saying;
they did not yet understand
what he was doing.

After the washing,
drying his hands,
putting the water aside
and his tunic on,
he said:
"Did you see what I was doing?
Did you see
how I, the master,
washed the feet of you,
my servants?

That is what you should do
to each other,
if you want to be like me,
if you want to commemorate me."
It was at this point
that both versions,
the one of Mark, Matthew, and Luke,
where bread is broken
and wine is shared,
coincide
with the version of John:
Do this
to commemorate me.

The *this* he was speaking about
was not only
the breaking of that bread;
it was not only
the sharing of that wine;
it was also the washing of those feet,
the service
he rendered them,
the service he had been rendering them
all the time,
healing the sick,
making the blind see,
making the deaf hear,
making peace,
establishing the kingdom of God
here on earth,
among them.
Traditionally
the feast of Corpus Christi
seems to invite us
to be
in front of the tabernacle
on our knees,
to adore, to pray,
and to worship,
or to carry that host

high on our shoulders
through our streets and parks.
That is not bad;
it is good;
maybe it should be done more often
by us.
> But we should not forget,
> we should never forget,
> that the host we are adoring
> is there *only*,
> ultimately,
> to be eaten,
> to disappear in the stomach
> of a human being
> who through the act of that eating
> gets Jesus Christ,
> his life
> and activity
> into himself,
> into herself.
> It is that life,
> that activity,
> that should make us live
> and "tick"
> as he lived
> and "ticked,"
> willing to wash the feet
> of all the others!

You could say it also
in unforgivable,
modern jargon:
when we receive him
we receive an *action-pack*
that should explode
in us
to make us
heal the sickness of this world,
open the ears of those who are deaf,
and the eyes of those who are blind,

cooperating
in the establishment of
the kingdom to come.
    Do you see now
    how important it is
    to consider his presence
    in the bread and wine
    as real?
    It is!

30.

THE GOOD IN YOU

2 Samuel 12:7–10, 13
Galatians 2:16, 19–21
Luke 7:36–8:3

Jesus was invited by a Pharisee.
His host had surrounded himself
with friends,
professional religious people,
the leaders
of the religiosity
in their country.
    Though invited,
    Jesus was not
    well treated by his host.
    He had received his professional friends
    better
    than this prophet
    from the street.
    Their feet had been washed,
    his feet had not been washed;
    they had been embraced when they entered,
    he had not been greeted at all;
    they had been welcomed,
    but Jesus had just been allowed
    to come in,

  that commoner from Nazareth,
  uneducated and very strange,
  with some extraordinary ideas
  about himself.
When they were at table
a woman came in,
a woman with a bad name in town.
They all knew about that bad name;
they all knew about her.
Did she arrive in the midst
of some of her customers
lying around that table?
Who knows?
  She went to Jesus.
  She had with her a bottle of perfume;
  had it been the gift from one of her clients?
  Had it been,
  maybe,
  the gift from one of them?
  She touched him;
  she wept,
  dried the tears
  that had dripped on his feet,
  and anointed them,
  expressing in that way
  her love, her respect, her faith.
Simon, seeing all this,
thought to himself:
"If this man were a prophet,
he would know who that woman is;
he would never allow her
to express herself like that."
  In that same stream of thought
  Simon indicated
  that he,
  the professional religious specialist,
  could not believe
  that there was the possibility of anything of value
  in that woman,

and at the same time
that there was,
as he always had been thinking,
nothing of any prophetic or religious value
in Jesus either.
That is why he said
to himself,
together with the others around him:
"How would this Jesus
be able to do anything
in the name of God?"
Simon, the Pharisee,
had a very low opinion
of the spiritual content
of his guests,
the invited one,
Jesus,
the uninvited one,
that woman.
In the same way we
have a very low opinion of the spiritual possibilities
of the people around us,
and of ourselves too,
conditioned as we are,
even nowadays,
by the professional religious leaders
around us.
    Some days ago
    we had a theological discussion;
    the topic was "The Holy Spirit."
    We asked each other
    whether we knew about the work
    of the Holy Spirit
    in our own experience.
    It was strange
    but at first almost everybody
    spoke about *others* healing,
                    making peace,
                    speaking in tongues,

and it was only after some time,
that someone said:
"Why are we only looking
for the extraordinary things
done by others?"
And slowly, slowly, slowly,
we ourselves started to remember
events in our own lives:
peacemaking,
sharing,
healing,
forgiveness,
communication.
Some months ago
I was in a primary school.
There too we were speaking about the Holy Spirit
in us.
I asked the children in front of me:
"Did you ever do anything good
in your lives?"
They all looked at me
with their enormous eyes,
and said almost spontaneously
and in chorus:
"No!"
      Was this a reflection
      of the opinion of their professional leaders
      at home,
      their parents,
      saying all day:
      "You are no good"?
It was only after some time
that one small boy remembered:
"Oh, yeah!
I helped an old lady
cross the street."
And a girl said:
"I had one piece of candy
and I broke it in half

to give a piece to my friend.
I think that was good.''
    I then asked:
    ''Did your parents
    ever do anything good?''
    And again they all said,
    spontaneously and in chorus:
    ''No, never.''
    I said:
    ''Now listen, think carefully.''
    One boy looked up
    and said:
    ''My father?
    Something really good?
    No, never.''
        After some minutes
        they remembered:
        my breakfast is always ready in the morning,
        my mother tells me a story every evening,
        my father brings me to bed,
        sometimes,
        my mothers sews for the poor. . . .
Simon the church leader
thought:
''Look at her sins.''
Jesus told Simon:
''No, look at her goodness.
You did not greet me,
she did;
you did not wash my feet,
she did;
you did not kiss me,
she did;
you did not respect me,
she does!''
    And turning to the woman
    ''Don't listen to him;
    forget about the evil in you;
    think of the good.
    I do.''

Simon had a low opinion
of that woman;
Simon had a low opinion
of Jesus.
According to him and his friends
they were too common
to have any good in them.
    Under their influence
    very many must have had
    a very low opinion
    of their own spiritual possibilities.
We often have that too.
We too are taught not to take ourselves
too seriously
when it comes to our potentialities in the Spirit.
    One of the things
    Jesus wanted to do in our lives
    is to clarify
    that very issue.
    He did it for that woman;
    he wants to do it for all of us.
Let us be convinced by him.
Anyone who thinks lowly of herself or himself
cannot do the great things
we are created for.

31.

SUNDAY AFTER SUNDAY

Zechariah 12:10–11
Galatians 3:26–29
Luke 9:18–24

Brothers and sisters,
is it not remarkable
that you are willing to come together
Sunday after Sunday after Sunday
to church
to listen to the story
of a person who suffered so much
in all kinds of ways?
    Why do you do this?
    Why do we do this?
    Don't we hear sufficient stories of suffering?
    Is not the whole world full of those stories?
    Aren't the papers full of them?
    Don't we hear them all the time over the radio?
    Don't we see them over the television?
    Don't we all have our sad stories,
    stories about what happened during our youth,
    stories about our parents,
    stories about our children,
    stories about our friends,

154

stories about ourselves,
stories about others:
> a painful sickness,
> an unjust treatment,
> a terrible scandal,
> a degrading death?

I think that it is not exaggerating to say
that in the life-story of each human being
you find such a story,
even in the lives of those
who always seem to be joyful
and to smile.
And I am sure that you have yours;
when you are young
maybe you are not yet able
to tell it correctly
or freely,
to yourself or others;
but the older you become
the more aware you will be of your pain,
until you find someone
who is willing to listen to you,
and telling your story
you yourself will
discover the tale of your woes.

> But so often it is very difficult
> to find someone who listens,
> who really listens,
> who really takes the time and the courage
> to listen to you.

You remember that person who wanted to tell you
his story, her story?
Do you remember how you dodged him,
how you dodged her,
thinking:
*"My load is heavy enough,
I don't want to carry the load of others"*?

> How often did you not experience
> that nobody was willing to listen to you

when you wanted so much to talk
to someone.
And now you are here,
to listen once more
to the story
about *his* arrest,
  his detention,
  his suffering,
  and *his* death.
Why?
Is it maybe
because you are consoled
by what he said at the beginning
of his suffering:
"Father, not my will, but yours be done"?
Is it maybe
because you feel comforted
by his last words
while he was suffering:
"Father into your hands I commend my Spirit"?
Is it maybe
because you like to hear
how after his death
he rose, appeared for a few days,
and then disappeared for good to be in heavenly bliss?
  Maybe,
  but all this sounds like resignation,
  like hiding yourself completely away
  and forgetting about yourself
  in view of heaven
  in view of a pie in the sky!
At first hearing
that is what Jesus himself seems to ask
in the gospel:
"If anyone wants to be
a follower of me,
let him renounce himself
and take up his cross
and follow me."

That is what he did;
he renounced himself
and carried his cross,
but *not* in a passive way,
not without a reason,
not without an intention,
not like a passive puppet in the hands of his Father
or the people around him.
That is what he did
in an *active* way,
knowing perfectly well
that his attempts to establish a just and good world
here on earth
would cause him suffering
and finally death.
He did *not* say
"my blood is going to *be shed*."
He said,
"My blood is going to be shed
for you,
for the sake of justice,
a better human society,
the year of grace,
the establishment of God's kingdom."

    He knew what he wanted;
    he knew the price;
    he understood that it would have to be paid in
    suffering
    and he accepted that fact.
That seems to be the best reason
to hear, again and again,
the story of his suffering,
his death and resurrection.
His suffering made sense to him
because he saw it as a result of his
work for the kingdom in this world.

    In the same way so much of our suffering
    makes sense
    when we see it in that light.

Our sufferings,
your sufferings,
is the price,
should be the price
we pay
for our efforts to change the world.
Jesus tells us,
"If you are my follower,
take up the cross
you will have to bear
if you are with me
in my attempts
to change this world,
to make it a just place,
to make it a holy place,
to make it a good place to live in for all.
It is that cross
we should be willing to carry.
It is that suffering
we should be willing to take upon
ourselves
in view of
the kingdom of God,
here and now.
Isn't it in that way
that all our suffering
makes sense?
Isn't that,
maybe,
what we wanted to hear?

32.

CALLED TO LIBERTY

1 Kings 19:16, 19–20
Galatians 4:31–5:1, 13–18
Luke 9:51–62

Paul wrote:
"He freed us."
He meant to free us
for ever.
Paul even added:
"No law can touch you!"
    We might wonder
    what this freedom really means.
    He liberated us
    through his death on the cross,
    many will repeat,
    thinking of a sacrifice,
    a price, a ransom,
    paid for us.
Some get very enthusiastic
about this.
They burst out in chant and dance,
witnessing to it.
They fill radio and television programs
with it endlessly.

But is that endlessness in itself
    not a sign
    that they too
    are slightly confused,
    and don't know
    what really happened
    to them?
We could look
at this liberation,
maybe,
from another point of view.
In Jesus
our human possibilities
become visible.
He showed
what it means
to be a human being.
He showed
what it means to live from within:
    a life
    that made him,
    according to the gospel of today,
    resolutely take
    the road to Jerusalem,
    though he foresaw,
    and foretold
    what would happen
    to him once in that town.
He also taught them
the conditions
that have to be fulfilled
before
we reach his level
of inner liberty:
    no nest,
    no hole,
    no resting place,
    no time for the past:
    "let the dead bury their dead";

no time
for the present:
"no goodbye for the family at home";
completely open
towards the kingdom of God,
without ever looking back.
  That is a strange message
  in the mouth of a leader.
  They rarely grant,
  if ever,
  such a liberty,
  such a dignity,
  such a responsibility
  to others.
It is what Paul
understood
better than anyone else.
Wasn't he the one
who broke most radically
with his past and his present?
Wasn't he the one
who was
in conflict about
that past and that present
with a leader
like Peter?
  Paul also knew best
  the dangers:
  "You were called to liberty,
  not in view of self-indulgence,
  but to serve and love each other,
  building the new community."
We are free to love;
we are free to serve;
we are not bound up;
we are not closed;
we are not chained;
we are free
in the Lord.

33.

SEVENTY-TWO

Isaiah 66:10–14
Galatians 6:14–18
Luke 10:1–12, 17–20

I met a Jewish scholar,
a real Jewish scholar.
We spoke about religious issues;
being a real Jewish scholar
he obviously was very interested
in those issues.
We spoke about Jesus;
we spoke about Paul;
we spoke about the Bible;
we spoke about scholarship;
and then he said:
      "You Christians,
      you are lacking in biblical scholarship;
      you very rarely get the real meaning
      even of what Jesus said,
      or of what Paul wrote,
      because you simply don't sufficiently know
      their Jewish background."
I thought about this
when the gospel of today

mentions that Jesus
sent out seventy-two of his disciples.
Seventy-two,
why seventy-two?
And he is sending them out
in view of a harvest;
he sends them out
to reap and collect,
to bring together and gather.

    Why seventy-two?
    I tried to find out
    in some scholarly works
    and I found an answer,
    an answer that makes the gospel of today
    a very revealing,
    a very interesting,
    and a very relevant one.

If you count
in the first book of the Bible, Genesis,
all the sons
of Noah's children, Sem, Cham, and Japhet,
you come to
seventy-two.
The Bible tells
how after the flood
seventy-two peoples
started to spread
all over the world.
Those seventy-two
represent all the peoples
of the earth.

    All peoples,
    though they now have
    more than seventy-two names,
    and though you can count them now
    in their thousands,
    go back
    to that original start
    of seventy-two.

Read from this point of view,
read with this background:
Luke tells us
that when Jesus sent out those seventy-two
he must have been thinking
of those seventy-two sons,
of those seventy-two ancestors,
of those seventy-two peoples,
of all peoples
in this world.

     Those seventy-two
     got a mission from Jesus,
     a very clear mission.
     They had to announce,
     "The kingdom of God
     is very near."

And you know
what the kingdom of God entails;
it means that sometime all peoples
will join
to one banquet
prepared for all of them
by their parent
and life-origin
in heaven.

     That is not all Jesus said;
     Jesus also said
     that they should consider themselves
     as laborers
     bringing in a harvest.
     And he added that
     the harvest is rich,
     the harvest is ripe,
     the harvest is ready,
     the plants in the field,
     the ears in the wheat,
     the corn on the cob,
     the potatoes in the dark under the earth,
     the grapes shining in the sun,

the oranges on the trees,
the bananas between their leaves,
they are all ready to be
collected,
but the laborers are
few.
Brothers and sisters,
dear friends,
do you see
what this means?
It means that,
according to Jesus,
within all our cultures
movements and developments
have taken place
that make us
hunger and thirst
for that meal
we will have together
with our Father in heaven,
with God,
who as a mother,
the mother in the first reading of today,
wants to comfort
her child:
humanity.

    It is Paul,
the apostle of the nations,
who understood this best.
Preaching in Athens
he said,
referring to the same Genesis passage:
"From one human being
he created all races of humankind
and made them live
throughout the whole earth.
He himself fixed beforehand
the exact times and the limits of the places
where they would live.

He did this
so that they would look for him
and find him
as they felt about for him.''
Those seventy-two were sent
to gather all of them,
to collect the harvest
and bring it home.
We are sent out
in the same way,
and that is why all of us,
to whatever culture we belong,
should be gatherers
and peacemakers.
We are of the seventy-two.

34.

FROM WITHIN

Deuteronomy 30:10–14
Colossians 1:15–20
Luke 10:25–37

Moses wrote:
"This law is not
beyond your strength
or beyond your reach.
It is not in heaven;
it is not beyond the seas.
No, it is very near to you.
It is in your mouth;
it is in your heart."
　　These words
　　Jesus took very much
　　to heart;
　　these words
　　he applied
　　before referring
　　to anything else.
　　These words
　　made him look
　　for his Father's Spirit
　　in anyone he met,

bringing out
what so often
seemed to be lost.
A lawyer came to him
to ask:
"What should I do
to inherit eternal life?"
Jesus answered:
"What should you do,
to inherit eternal life?"
and the man gave his answer,
not from within,
but from without,
from the law he knew so well:
    "You must love
    the Lord your God
    with all your heart,
    with all your soul,
    with all your strength,
    with all your mind,
    and your neighbor
    as yourself."
"You have answered right,"
Jesus said.
"Do this
and life is yours."
    The lawyer then
    came with another question,
    a tricky one,
    a dangerous one,
    "And who is my neighbor?"
    It was a tricky question
    and a dangerous one
    because Jesus had been accused
    of going further than the law;
    and isn't going further
    than the law
    going against
    that law?

The law originally restricted
the idea of neighbor
to the members of the Jewish people
and the strangers living
in their country only.
In the time of Jesus,
the group of those strangers
had, however, been further reduced
to proselytes
only,
drawing around their people
an impenetrable magical ring.
      What answer
      would Jesus,
      seen with Romans and pagans,
      healing those Romans and pagans,
      give?
      None;
      he told a story.
It was the story
about a Jew
walking from Jerusalem to Jericho
who was beaten up on his way
and left behind,
bruised, crippled,
and slowly bleeding to death.
A Jew came along,
and passed;
another Jew came along,
and passed;
a Samaritan,
no Jew,
no proselyte,
no neighbor,
came along and stopped.
He bound off the bleeding;
he dressed the wounds;
he poured oil and wine
on the dressings;

he brought him
to a country inn
for further treatment,
guaranteeing the payment
of all the costs
involved.
>When the story was over,
>Jesus asked the lawyer:
>"Who was the neighbor
>of that man who was beaten up
>alongside the road?"
He thought of the ring,
the magical ring
his people had been drawing around itself;
he thought about the law,
the written law
as customarily explained
in a very restrictive way,
and yet,
notwithstanding
all that legal and documented pressure
from without,
he said from *within*,
from within himself:
>"The one who took pity
>on him!"
>breaking in that way
>from within himself,
>the magical spell.
>He did it from within,
>from within!
And Jesus had found
what had been
lost.

35.

HIS LOVE AND TENDERNESS

Genesis 18:1–10
Colossians 1:24–28
Luke 10:38–42

You remember
how we were confronted with the good Samaritan,
that stranger
who got off his donkey
to help someone.
You remember how Jesus told that story
to explain
who our neighbor is.
     Our neighbor
     is the stranger,
     the man alongside the road,
     the refugee,
     the runaway child,
     the young prostitute,
     the drunkard who fell in the street.
It is as if Jesus
sends us all in this world,
as one enormous
aid organization,
to clear our neighborly mess
  at that level.

Some people take him very seriously
in all this,
sometimes even too seriously.
They are so busy
that they never have time
for themselves;
they are so busy
that they never have time
for the ones around them.
I knew a family
far from here
who had a father
who really lived the story of that Samaritan.
He was always busy;
he was always helping others;
he was a member of all kinds of organizations
trying to improve
the lot of suffering humankind;
he really had made a 100 percent option
for the poor.
But because of that
he had never any time
for his wife;
he never had any time
to sit down with his children;
he was always busy
day and night
with the ones
alongside the road.
One day his daughter of fourteen
wanted to talk to him
about something very important,
but every time she asked her father to listen to her,
her father
had no time to sit down;
he was busy,
again and again.
She went to her mother
asking her what to do,

and her mother said:
"Undo your hair,
put some dirt on your face,
dress in some rags,
walk barefooted,
and knock at his office door,
and you will see that
he will receive you
and listen
because he will consider you
to be a stranger."
     That is what she did.
     Her father, of course,
     recognized her immediately,
     but he understood
     and sat down.
That is what Mary did.
She sat down
with him.
     The gospel of today
     follows the story of that good Samaritan.
     Jesus comes to a village.
     A woman, Martha, comes out of her house
     and, like that good Samaritan,
     she invites him
     into her house.
     Like that Samaritan
     she starts to get active,
     very active;
     and in no time the water is boiling,
     nice smells come out of the kitchen,
     she is running up and down,
     laying the table,
     busy, busy, busy:
          no time to sit down,
          no time to rest,
          no time to listen.
Her younger sister Mary
does sit down,

and with great, nice, wide-open eyes,
and with very open ears,
she sits at the feet of Jesus
lovingly
and attentively.
        Martha comes out of the kitchen;
        she stands in front of them;
        she remains standing
        and says:
        "Can't you tell my sister
        to help me?"
And Jesus says:
"Martha, Martha,
you are so busy,
but Mary chose
the better part."
        The gospel of today
        is an amendment
        to the story of the good Samaritan.
        It wants to show
        that love of neighbor
        does not only express itself
        in concrete help to strangers;
        it shows that love to neighbor
        means attention,
        intimacy,
        and tenderness.
Dag Hammerskjoeld,
who was for years the Secretary General
of the United Nations,
wrote in his diary:
        "People who are worried about
        the world issues,
        about the global problems,
        and who are busy with those problems,
        very easily forget
        the smaller issues.
        If you are not willing to be good
        in the smaller circle
        of your family and friends,

you can't do anything
for humanity as such.
Without that intimacy,
you live in a world of abstractions,
in which your solipsism,
your hunger for power,
your destructive tendencies,
maim their only more powerful opponent:
love."
It is better to be good
with all one's heart
to one person
than to sacrifice
oneself
for the whole of humanity.
    Jesus did both;
    that is why he sat down
    with Mary,
    and again
    he is our model
    for all time to come.

36.

HIS RESERVEDNESS

Genesis 18:20–32
Colossians 2:12–14
Luke 11:1–13

They saw him praying.
There must have been something very special
about his prayer.
That is why they asked him:
"Teach us how to pray,
teach us to pray
as you are doing it."
You just heard his answer
in the gospel reading.
But there is more to that answer
than just
saying the Our Father.
> The gospels speak often about Jesus praying,
> but they do not mention
> all his prayers.
> They mention that he went
> to participate
> in the Easter feast at Jerusalem;
> they never speak about his participation
> in the liturgical prayers there.

176

We are told
that he went every Sabbathday
to the synagogue
while living in Nazareth;
but there is no mention
of his prayers in that synagogue.
We hear how he lived
very piously
in the circle of his family;
but there is no trace
of his family prayers.
What is mentioned
is special,
is personal:
he went to the desert
and to the mountain tops to pray.
What is mentioned
is that he said:
"Enter your innerroom
as you pray to the Father
who is there hidden."
What is mentioned
is that he warned:
"Don't pray as the Pharisees
who pray in public to be seen
by all."

Another characteristic
is his *reservedness*
in his prayers.
He refuses to invoke the power of God
as we so often do
when in difficulties or need.
When a man hurt him
in front of the approving high priests,
he said:
"Don't you realize
that I could call on my Father for help
and that he would send me at once
more than twelve armies of angels
to defend me?"

But he doesn't do it,
not even when he is caught
in such difficulties and harassment
that he has to shout in anguish:
"My God, my God,
why did you forsake me?"
Why did he not pray
as all of us would be tempted to pray,
as so many of them had prayed in the Bible:
"Bash their heads;
let their children perish;
make their women infertile;
let the hills and the mountains
fall over them!"

Was that, maybe, the reason
that we don't hear anything,
about him joining
the old prayers in their temple
and their synagogues?

He was sure
that God would have helped him;
he was sure that God would have interfered
with power and might
against those who used power against him,
but he did not ask for that type of violence.

He asked God
not to use power;
he said
while they were nailing him on the cross:
"Father,
please don't look;
don't see;
they don't know
what they are doing."

How could the circle of violence
he came to break through
in this world
ever be broken through
by him using violence,

even the power
of his Father?
And that is what he taught them
when he said,
when you pray
say:

   Our Father,
         not the Father of me and my group,
         but OUR Father,
         who can't be turned against anyone,
   thy kingdom come,
   thy will be done,
         not in power
         but in the growth
         we are now asking for,
         respecting our human decisions,
   and give US bread,
         all of us,
         not to some,
         but to all,
   and help US to forgive,
         not using violent revenge
         but the forgiveness
         that liberates us from the past,
   as you forgive
   and lead us no longer in temptation
   to do otherwise.
   Amen.

37.

NOT A DAYFLY

Ecclesiastes 1:2; 2:21–23
Colossians 3:5, 9–11
Luke 12:13–21

Two of the readings tonight
are about the uselessness,
the vanity of life.
  When you are young you don't notice that
  so much.
  You are thinking about the future;
  you are thinking about your career;
  you are thinking about all you are going to do,
  though nowadays even some young people ask:
  "Why was I born?
  What can I do?
  What is the meaning of it all?"
  and that is very sad.
When you are middle-aged
you are very often too busy
to think about things like the vanity of life;
there are too many worries;
there are too many problems;
you forget about all the rest,
God and religion included.

It is especially when you get older,
when you look back,
that the vanity of all you did
might suddenly hit you,
making you feel very depressed,
and that you might say
with the author of that Bible book Ecclesiastes:
"Vanity of vanity,
all is vanity,
emptiness, emptiness,
all is empty;
for anyone who toils with wisdom,
knowledge, and skill must leave it all to a man
who has spent no labor on it.
This too is emptiness and utterly wrong.
What reward has a man for all his labor,
his scheming, and his toil
under the sun?

 All during his life
 a businessman's work is pain
 and vexation to him;
  even at night his mind knows no rest.
 This too is emptiness."

I don't know whether you have ever heard
about dayflies.
There are very many varieties of them.
A dayfly is a fly
that is born early in the morning
at about seven o'clock
just when the sun starts to warm up the earth,
and it will die before the sun sets
at the end of the day.
A dayfly lives only
twelve hours.

 One day the sun shone
 on a small lump of dayfly eggs
 somewhere here in Kenya.
 The little eggs opened one by one,
 not all at the same time.

It was a quarter past seven
when the egg of our dayfly
Joachim opened.
He was a bit late
when he came out of his egg.
A lot of brothers and sisters
were already flying around.
When Joachim came out of his egg
he felt confused.
He was very wet
and his wings were crinkled,
but about ten minutes later he was dried up,
his wings opened up nicely,
and by half past seven he was flying around,
looking for food,
as he saw his brothers and sisters do.
By half past eight he suddenly started to grow;
he got very long legs,
and very long wings.
He felt a bit unhappy about it;
he did not like the sight of himself in the mirror.
His brothers and sisters told him,
"Don't worry,
it will pass;
it is your puberty."
By nine he started to look around for a friend,
not a boy friend.
He did it very shyly
because every time he saw a girl
he started to blush
very deeply.
He did not like that
and he would fly away.
By ten he had found a girlfriend,
a pretty one,
and he introduced her
to the older members of his family,
those who were born twenty minutes before him.
They disagreed;

they said you can't marry that girl,
she is not of our class,
she is not of our standing,
she does not have your color,
you would not be able to be happy with her all your life;
forget about her.
But he could not.
They continued meeting each other stealthily;
it became twelve o'clock;
it became half past twelve.
He was getting older, and she too,
and finally she said to him,
"If you still want me to lay any eggs for you,
you will have to be quick in marrying me;
otherwise it will be too late;
and so they married
notwithstanding the family opposition.
She laid her first eggs by half past one.
There were some complications
because she really had got a little bit too old
to do that for the first time.
By two Joachim was at the top of his career,
but by three,
some young ones,
born about twenty minutes later than he,
started to gossip and to complain.
They said:
"Should he not give us a chance,
should he not make place for the younger ones?"
That is why he resigned at
four o'clock.
He started to feel a bit old.
His wife died rather soon after,
at about half past four.
She really had laid her first eggs a bit too late.
By half past five
old age really set in;
he got a bad liver
and rheumatism in his left hind leg.

By six o'clock he felt like dying
but the younger members of the family said:
"You are too young for that;
you have still at least 60 minutes to live."
It did not help.
By half past six he died.
    And everyone asked:
    "Why did he live,
    why did he live so short a time?
    He came and he went,
    what for?"
    Vanity of vanity,
    emptiness of emptiness.
Of course you are not a dayfly;
you live much longer.
If we become seventy,
and I hope that all of us become at least that old,
we will have lived not twelve
but exactly
six hundred eleven thousand five hundred twenty hours.
But yet
is our story
not as meaningless as the one of Joachim
the dayfly?
Isn't that what the holy book
seems to say?
Isn't that what many preachers repeat?
    But they are wrong.
    Our lives can be in vain,
    that is true.
    The gospel of today tells us of such a useless life.
    There was that man
    who suddenly got such a rich harvest
    that he felt very poor
    because his barns were too small.
    So he destroyed his old barns;
    he constructed new ones;
    he collected all he had in that storage
    and then he started to speak to himself,

and he said
not to others, but to his heart:
    "My love, my dove,
    now you can rest,
    now you can eat,
    now you can drink,
    now you can enjoy,
    now you are safe."
And that was all;
he did not think about anything else.
He really lived like that dayfly
though he lived, if he became seventy,
611,510 hours longer.
Then God started to speak,
and God said to him:
"Fool,
is that all you can think about?
Don't you realize that I come to take you away tonight?
Don't you realize that you should live in another way,
making yourself rich in the sight of God
by good works,
by working for justice and peace,
working at the establishment of my kingdom?"
    It happens very often
    that people ask,
    "Why was I born,
    why do I live,
    what is the meaning of my life?"
Maybe you are asking that question too,
and there is no answer to that question
when you are alone,
thinking of yourself alone;
there is not even an answer to that question
when you are with many,
but without God.
    It is when you relate to those others,
    it is when you relate to God,
    that your life is not in vain,
    and that it is not true to say:

"Vanity of vanity,
all is vanity."
We are not dayflies.
We should not be like them.
Amen.

38.

NO NEED TO BE AFRAID

Wisdom 18:6–9
Hebrews 11:1–2, 8–19
Luke 12:32–48

We live in difficult days.
The days of glamor are over,
the days of snug security too.
What we were able to do ten years ago,
we can't do anymore.
It is as if things are getting
more and more complicated.
The travels we could make without any fear,
all over the world,
came to an end.
The evening walks we could make without any harassment
can't be made anymore.
There are dangers everywhere:
in international conflicts,
in the national security states,
the muggers around the corners
of our very own streets and squares.
Almost every week
there are rumors of new wars;

almost every day
new conflicts seem to break out.
And even if we aren't directly involved
in all this,
everyone is hit.
We are all paying the price.
Even the most common staple foods
are priced beyond reach
to pay for the armaments
they say
we need.

    And in all this,
    through all this,
    the gospel maintains:
    "There is no need to be afraid,
    little flock,
    for it has pleased your Father
    to give you the kingdom."

A promise,
nothing more,
is the only thing
we seem to have.
Nothing else.
Is that sufficient
to help us survive,
for us to hang on to,
to make us be motivated enough
to continue?

    For Abraham it was,
    as you heard in the second reading of today.
    Because of such a promise
    Abraham left the town in which he was living;
    because of such a promise
    he started to live as a nomad,
    in a tent,
    always on his way,
    looking forward to a city
    founded, designed, and built
    by God.

He never saw that city;
he never arrived at it;
his whole life was full of complications;
he had very good reasons to doubt.
Hadn't he been promised
a descendancy as numerous as the stars,
and yet, almost up to the moment of his death,
he had no child,
and when he finally had his child,
he was asked to sacrifice it
to God.
> But he kept on
> because of his dream,
> because of that promise,
> because of that town,
> because of a settlement
>> he never saw realized in his life.
Abraham
is a good example
of what a promise
can do
in the life of a man.
> Aren't we in the same situation?
> Have we anything more than a promise?
> Yes, we have.
> We are further;
> we are nearer;
> we have a tangible model;
> we have the fulfillment
> with us.
We have it in a celebration like this one;
we realize here and now
what we cannot realize as yet
in everyday life,
but here it is,
here we have it.
It sometimes happens in a congregation like this
that two families
really dislike, even hate each other.

They never shake hands;
their children are told not to play with each other;
they never say a word to each other;
they don't even look at each other;
they are air,
very thin air,
a kind of polluted air
to each other.
>When they enter church
>the first thing they do
>is look
>where the others are sitting.
>When they are sitting to the right,
>the others go to the left;
>when they are sitting to the left,
>the others go to the right.
There will be no prayer for each other;
there will be no exchange of a greeting;
there will be no kiss of peace.
But then
at the moment of the sharing of the bread,
they both go
to the same table;
they both receive the same Lord;
they both share the same wine;
they both form together
the one body of Jesus Christ.
>"There is no need to be afraid,
>little flock,
>for it has pleased your Father
>to give you the kingdom!"
>Not in a promise only,
>but a reality here and now,
>not fully real,
>but nevertheless
>the model of a better future.

39.

ASSUMPTION IS ACCEPTANCE

Revelation 11:19; 12:1–6, 10
1 Corinthians 15:20–26
Luke 1:39–56

Isn't it strange
that we get as our gospel reading today,
at this feast of the assumption
of the Blessed Virgin Mary into heaven,
the meeting between Mary and Elizabeth?
> That meeting does not seem to have
> anything heavenly about it
> at all.
> An aunt and a niece
> meet each other.
> The heavenliness in the story
> seems to depend
> on their heaviness;
> they are both filled with
> something from heaven:
> Mary with Jesus,
> Elizabeth with John.

191

Yet, brothers and sisters,
it is from that meeting
that we might learn
what this feast of the assumption
can mean
and does mean.
     When those two women meet each other,
     they do it in a special way.
     They admire each other.
     They admire each other
     not in a way
     that creates a distance between them,
     but in a way that brings them
     very near to each other.
     They embrace each other;
     they lay hands on each other,
     and they say:
     "You, that you are here,
     that you came to me,
     you of whom I think so highly,
     how glad I am that you came!"
They meet like friends,
no power play,
no false pretenses,
no jealousy,
no hidden motives,
open and clear,
attention for each other,
and joy,
acceptance,
friendship.
     Elizabeth is so touched
     that she reacts with her whole person,
     not only spiritually,
     but with her body too:
     the fruit
     she is carrying in her womb
     jumps up
     with joy.

And Mary,
Mary reacts
in the same way.
She opens her mouth
and sings:
>about herself,
>about her place,
>about being small,
>about being great,
>about her God,
>about her thanks,
>*about being accepted*
>*by God*,
>as a human being,
>as a person,
>as a woman,
>as a mother,
>with *spirit* and *body*.

We might come to
very many moralizing conclusions:
that this is the manner
we should meet each other;
that this is the only way
of giving each other the opportunity
to find our place
in this world,
and in God's plan.
>But that does not seem to be the point
>today.
>The point today
>is
>the assumption,
>that acceptance of Mary,
>by God,
>with her whole mind,
>with her whole spirit.

God did not use her;
she was neither God's vehicle,
nor God's means;

she was she;
she was accepted
as she had been made
with her strengths,
and her weaknesses
    —because she too,
    now and then,
    was in doubt,
    angry,
    upset,
    and afraid.
What Elizabeth did to Mary
and Mary to Elizabeth
at that very simple meeting
somewhere in the holy land's bush
is what God did to her,
the mother of Jesus.
    Celebrating this,
    we should take her
    as our MODEL:
    that is how we are treated by God,
    that is how we are going to be treated
    by her son.

40.

WHERE DO YOU COME FROM?

Jeremiah 38:4–6, 8–10
Hebrews 12:1–4
Luke 12:49–53

There is something very strange
about the gospel of today,
something so strange
that you must have been struck by it too,
if you came to think of it.
Let me explain
what I mean.
>   There is that wedding feast.
>   It has been going on
>   already for quite some time;
>   many guests have arrived;
>   the party is in full swing;
>   the doors are closed
>   to keep gate-crashers out;
>   as an extra precaution
>   there are powerful ushers
>   watching those doors.
Then, suddenly,
there is a knock at the door.
The bridegroom is informed;

he goes to the door;
the ushers stand ready;
he opens the door
only a crack,
and he sees some people outside.
He looks at them
and he does not say:
"I don't know you;
you can't come in."
Instead he says:
"I don't know where
you are coming from.
Go away!"
> It seems that he knows them;
> it is obvious that he does not like them,
> and to express his dislike
> he says:
> "I don't know
> where you are coming from."
> or maybe he says:
> "I don't know
> what you have been doing."
He knows them
because the people at the door say:
"But, listen,
we ate with you;
we drank with you;
we listened to you in our streets.
Don't be silly.
Don't you recognize us?"
> Again he answers:
> "Where do you come from?"
> And now he even goes further,
> as he adds:
> "Get away from me,
> *you wicked men!*"
While he is speaking to them,
they can look
through the crack of the door;

they can see
who are sitting at his table;
they can see
who are dancing around;
they can see
who had been allowed to enter;
they recognize:

> Abraham,
> Isaac,
> Jacob,
> and *all the prophets*
> of the kingdom of God,
> from the east, the west,
> the north, and the south.

It is in that way
that they got an insight about
why they did not qualify,
what they had not done,
why he said:
"I don't know
where you are coming from!"
They had been eating
with him,
yes;
they had been drinking
with him,
yes;
they had been listening
to him,
yes;
but had they been
prophets?

> By now
> all of us must know
> that a prophet is not one
> who tells the future.
> The prophet is the one
> who knows
> what way leads to the kingdom of God;

the prophet is the one
who knows
where justice is missing
and where justice can be found;
the prophet is someone
like Moses,
>who under very serious difficulties
>marched the people of God
>out of the misery and dependency of Egypt
>towards a new future.
That is where the prophets
come from;
that is where the prophets
are leading to.
It is not sufficient
to eat with him,
as we are going to do now;
it is not sufficient
to drink with him;
it is not sufficient
to listen to him
or to read the Bible;
it is not sufficient
to pray for his kingdom,
to realize his kingdom in a sign only,
to dream about it in community,
to wish each other justice and peace
during a liturgical celebration.
>We must be on our own feet,
>walking the way
>that leads from darkness to light,
>from misery to justice,
>from struggle to peace;
>and it is only
>when walking that way,
>that we will be
>invited,
>and that he will know
>where we are coming from!

41.

BE GENTLE IN YOUR BUSINESS

Ecclesiastes 3:17–18, 20, 28–29
Hebrews 12:18–19, 22–24
Luke 14:1, 7–14

The gospel of today
contradicts itself.
Twice advice is given,
and the two pieces of advice
contradict each other.
> It is as if Jesus says,
> "Go,"
> and at the same time,
> "Don't go."
> It is as if Jesus says,
> "Do this,"
> and at the same time,
> "Don't do this."
Let us start with the second saying.
He recommends:
"If you prepare a feast,
don't invite all kinds of guests
who can,

and who will,
repay you.
Don't calculate in that way,
but invite those who will not be able
to do anything in return.
Invite disinterestedly
and your feast will be grand.
If you invite only those
who are going to reinvite you
they will say to each other:
'He invited us
only because he wants something in return,'
and your feast will be
no feast
at all.
Be wise,
don't calculate,
be generous,
and all will go well."
     In his first piece of advice
     it seems
     that Jesus suggests
     calculation.
     He says:
     "If you want to be honored,
     don't take too high a place
     at table
     because you will be humiliated
     when the host comes in;
     don't even take the place
     that is yours
     because you will not be honored
     either.
     Think,
     calculate,
     be clever,
     take too low a place,
     and when the host comes in
     he will walk up to you,

    in front of all of them,
    and he will say:
    'Oh, don't sit there,
    come higher up.'
    And all the guests will say:
    'Look at him,
    what a noble man,
    and so humble.' "
There must have been something else
behind all this.
There must have been
a hidden intention,
and there is.
When we invite those
who cannot repay us,
our invitations
run according to the lines of the Father's heavenly banquet;
our invitations
run according to the lines of Jesus' kingdom.
    But isn't that true also
    when we sit down
    in this world
    with the poor and the smallest,
    with the miserable and the wretched,
    when we take their place,
    their stand,
    their position?
    Isn't that
    what he did?
And mind you,
this should not mean
that we all become
Sister Teresas of Calcutta,
or that we all start to hand out
what we have
to the poor.
    It doesn't even mean
    that we should begin
    all kinds of charitable associations.

All those are necessary now
because there is something else
we did not do,
the something else
indicated in the first reading of today:
>"My son and my daughter,
>*be gentle in carrying out*
>*your business,*
>*and you will be better loved*
>*than a lavish giver."*

Jesus Sirach advises us
to carry out our business
in the office,
in the family,
in the traffic,
in everything,
gently,
that is to say,
taking into account
the weak,
the poor,
the small,
and we will be loved better
because it is then
that the whole world
would change
to the extent
that all the aid,
that all the hand-outs,
would no longer be needed.
>Everyone,
>every single widow,
>every single orphan,
>and all the marginal ones,
>would find their
>place
>at the table of
>this world.

One of the great contemporary analyzers
of our modern world,
Karl Popper,
wrote
that society will only heal
when it takes the interest
of the weakest
of the weak
among us,
first.
In a third world country
we are accustomed
to aid,
to help,
to assistance
from the rich countries,
from outside,
from overseas,
but if those rich regions,
if those two other worlds,
would be more gentle
in their business,
if they would sit down with the poor
in the way Jesus suggested
and did,
would not everyone find
his and her place
here,
and in the kingdom
to come?

42.

HIS CROSS

Wisdom 9:13–19
Philemon 9–10, 12–17
Luke 14:25–33

You often meet people
who speak about their cross.
There was a husband
who came to complain about his wife.
He had all kinds of complaints:
she was lazy, he said;
she talked too much, he said;
she was not efficient at home, he said;
she spent too much money, he said;
she was a waste, he said;
she did not respect him, he said.

    And after that whole litany
    his face almost brightened up,
    and he added:
    "She is my cross
    in life."

And she came to complain;
he was lazy, she said;
he went too often to the bar with his friends, she said;
he was never at home, she said;

204

he kept a lot of money for himself, she said;
he was a waste, she said;
he did not respect her, she said.
    And then her face brightened up too,
    and she added:
    "He is my cross
    in life."
And they both thought
at that moment
of the cross above their marital bed
at home.
    Some speak about their cross
    because they have stomach ulcers,
    a headache, or a toothache,
    because they have not sufficient money
    to do what they would like to do;
    some speak about their cross
    because they failed in life,
    or they were not promoted in time
    and so on, and so on.
    Reading the gospel of today,
    we might wonder
    whether those are the things
    Christ meant
    when he said:
    "Anyone who does not carry
    his cross
    and come after me
    cannot be my disciple!"
Was he speaking about a stomach cramp,
about a toothache,
about a difficulty
in human relationships?
His cross seems to be
about something else,
and we should have a better look
at what he called
"my cross";

we should have a better look
at what brought him to
"his cross."
We all know
what brought him to his cross,
not his toothache,
though they had hit his teeth;
not his stomachache,
though he had terrible stomach spasms;
not his headache
though he was wearing that crown of thorns;
no, it was *his intent* in life,
it was what he wanted to do,
what he wanted to realize among us
in this world.
      We can describe his intentions
      in very different ways.
      We can say
      that he came to redeem us
      from sin,
      and that is true,
      very true;
      but we can also say
      the same
      in another way:
      he came to show us
      who we are,
      all of us.
      He came to tell us
      that once we discover
      our greatness,
      we will also discover
      that we should treat each other
      accordingly,
      equally,
      that the differences
      we make
      between ourselves
      because of sex,

because of color,
because of power,
because of money,
because of tribe or nation,
because of religion
are out,
and are wrong.
    And as everybody
    notices those differences,
    everybody turned
    against him
    at the end of his pilgrimage
    among us.
To walk on that way,
to march on that road
to justice,
and love,
and peace,
and unity,
will be for us
a way of the cross
too.
    Yet, that is what we are asked to do
    in our everyday life.
That is difficult,
you will say;
it is almost impossible,
you will say;
that is why it is your cross,
he will answer,
adding:
"Before you start doing it,
know what you are doing.
Don't start to build
without stones;
don't start the battle,
without the means;
don't make a fool of yourselves;
don't give scandal to others."

It is the way
to the cross.
It is the way
    where all preferences,
    all distinctions,
    all discriminations,
    all inequalities,
    all injustices,
    are given up,
    and even "hated."
It is the only way;
it is the royal road
leading
to the kingdom
itself.

43.

THE REAL LOST SON

Exodus 32:7–11, 13–14
1 Timothy 1:12–17
Luke 15:1–32

It is difficult to reflect
on the gospel of today.
It is too well known.
It does not seem to contain
any surprise element
any more.
It has been told millions and millions
of times,
over and over again.
It is one of the best known stories
in the Bible.
      That does not mean
      that it is well told.
      It does not mean
      that it is told
      in its context.
Who is the main person
in the story?
Because of whose behavior,
was the story told?

Because of the father?
Because of the younger son?
Because of the pig farmer?
Because of the servants?
Or because of the older son?
        Let us not forget
        that Jesus told the story
        to explain why he welcomed sinners
        and ate with them.
        He did this
        because the Pharisees and the scribes
        had been complaining
        about his doing so.
They never shook hands
with sinners;
they never greeted them;
they would undergo
all kinds of purification rites
if they ever touched
any of them;
and they definitely
would never welcome them
and eat with them
as he did.
        They did not understand
        Jesus' preference.
        Neither did they understand
        the Father's preference
        for his younger son
        because he too
        did not mind
        welcoming a sinner
        and preparing
        a meal for him.
They were like
the older brother
who did not care
about the younger one,

who did not share
his father's worries about him,
who refused to go in,
who refused to greet,
who refused to shake hands,
who refused to sit down
and eat with him.
    There is a story
    about a very old rabbi.
    One day a father came to him
    to complain about one of his two sons.
    He said:
    "My older one is so nice;
    my older one is so God-fearing;
    my older one is so respectful to me;
    my older son is my hope in life;
    but my younger son is so bad;
    my younger one respects
    neither God, nor man;
    my younger one will be my death.
    What should I do?"
The rabbi listened;
he even had closed his eyes
to listen better;
he was silent for quite some time
and then he said:
    "Your younger son
    needs your love most!"
That was the lesson
Jesus wanted to teach
those Pharisees and scribes.
That was the explanation
of his own attitude and behavior.
That is the lesson
he wanted to teach us
who so often have difficulties
while judging
others.

44.

THE BLOOD OF THE POOR

Amos 8:4–7
1 Timothy 2:1–8
Luke 16:1–13

Much has been said about money.
Much is going to be said about it
until the end of this world.
Some say
that everything can be bought
for money.
It is only a question
of its price.
Even Jesus was sold
for thirty pieces of silver,
the price of a slave
in that time.
"Money is the root of all evil"
is what scripture
says.
　　In the beginning of this century
　　there was a kind of prophet
　　living in France.
　　His name was
　　Léon Bloy,

though a name does not matter
in the case of a prophet.
He was like Amos
in the first reading of today
who describes how the rich
suck the poor
down to the point
that those poor are eating dirt
and are valued less
than a pair of sandals.
Bloy wrote a book in 1906.
He called the book
Money Is the Blood of the Poor,
a harsh,
an oversimplified,
a bitter,
a revolutionary,
but at the same time
a true statement.
Just think for a moment
about it.
Are not the rich countries
in the first and second worlds
at this very moment
so well off
because of the poverty
of third world
countries?

I come from a region
in the Netherlands
that was very, very poor
a century ago.
Its industry
was the poor man's industry:
textiles.
First the weavers were working
for almost nothing
in their own houses.

Then they started to work
in factories.
In my youth
there were still over 150 textile factories,
or textile related factories,
in the town I come from.
When you walked through it
it stank of boiling wool,
and the noise of the looms
was deafening.
The factory-owners were living
far out of town,
in beautiful residential areas.
    At the moment
    there are only two or three
    of those factories
    left.
    The town became too rich.
    This poor man's work
    was brought over to other countries,
    third world countries,
    where the pay is low,
    and the social provisions
    nil.
    Money is the poor man's blood.
Jesus said it in his way
in the gospel of today.
He says:
"Money,
that *thing*.
money,
that *tainted thing*."
He knew
that he would be sold
for it;
he knew
that his blood
would be bought
with it.

Nevertheless,
he does not say
to do away
with it.
He says
not to make it
your idol
because in that case
you will be tainted too,
and corrupt,
and rotten.
He says
to use it well,
to use it in such a way that,
though it will make your hands dirty,
you will be able to continue
to lift those very same hands
up to God
in prayer.
He knew
that it would be impossible
in our time,
in this world,
to do away with it.
And he comforts us,
he consoles us,
showing us
a way out.
He says
to use it well,
to use it to befriend the kingdom of God.
That does not mean
that our money should be given
to churches,
or to beggars,
or to poor people
just like that.
    It means
    that we should invest it

wisely
in the kingdom of God
here on earth,
a kingdom
that is nothing else
but human life.
We should invest it
not to satisfy the wants of some,
but the needs of all.
And then we can do
what Paul asks us all to do:
to lift up our hands,
though stained
by that tainted thing,
money,
praying
that one day
the kingdom may come,
>*and money may disappear,*
>so that all the blood
>will be washed away
>from our hands.
>Amen.

45.

THE POOR AT OUR DOOR

Amos 6:4–7
1 Timothy 6:11–16
Luke 16:19–31

We are all the rich man
of the gospel reading.
There is always someone poorer
than we
at our door-step.
     Some years ago,
     during a meeting of
     the World Council of Churches
     here in Nairobi,
     I had a visitor
     in the chaplaincy,
     a university professor of theology
     from Europe.
It was during the time
that the town was full with parking boys,
children of about ten or so
who had left school
after Standard Four
because in those days
the Government paid for their schooling
up to that standard only.

They surrounded the chaplaincy;
they camped around the chapel;
they even slept on its roof
to protect themselves against the dogs
of the city police.
There was a feeding program for them
on the other side of the street;
there was an informal school
here in the chapel.
Our guest saw all this;
he admired the work,
so he said;
but when the conference was over
after about two weeks or so,
he told me
that he was very glad to go home again
because, he said,
he wouldn't be able
to stand this confrontation
with poverty
all the time.
He went;
he escaped in a way,
but, of course,
he did not escape
at all.
He only made the distance
between his front door
and those poor
larger.
Though he was a very well-known
scholar,
he behaved like a child
who reasons:
"If I don't see you,
you don't exist,"
closing its eyes
not to see
the danger it fears.

All of us are rich
in comparison
with those
who are poorer
than we are.
All of us are lying on beds,
while others lie
in the gutters
alongside our lives.
> That is why all of us
> should listen carefully
> to the gospel of today.
> What should we do?
The gospel teaches
that to be rich
neither helps
in our salvation
nor in our relations with God.
> The gospel does not say either
> that the poverty of Lazarus
> brought him to heaven,
> nor that it gave him
> a special bond with God.
The gospel does not even tell
the rich
to hand out their riches
to the poor,
becoming poor themselves
in the process.
> The gospel teaches us
> something else,
> something totally different.
> When the rich man in hell
> asks Abraham to send Lazarus
> to his five brothers
> to warn them,
> Abraham answers
> that they should listen
> to Moses and the prophets.

They should listen to those
who tried to organize,
in the name of God,
a world
that would give a chance
to all,
a world
that would be arranged
in such a way
that everyone
would feel at home
and nobody would lie
at the door
of someone else.

    Those five brothers
    are we,
    still left behind.
    This instruction is meant
    for us,
    for all of us.

46.

YOUR FAITH SUFFICES

Habakkuk 1:2–3, 2:2–4
2 Timothy 1:6–8, 13–14
Luke 17:5–10

The gospels were written
for the first Christians.
They were written
to encourage them.
The gospel of Luke is no exception;
that gospel too
was written to encourage
the Christians Luke knew.
　　It is in this light
　　that we have to read
　　the gospel of today.
The people around Jesus went to him
and they told him:
"Please, give us some more faith;
we haven't enough of it;
we can't do anything as we are.
We can't even start.
Please help us.
We are very weak;
we are beginners;
you are so holy;

221

we aren't,
but we would love
to be like you.''
>They were like a businessman
>who says:
>''I don't have sufficient money;
>wait till I have some more
>and I will start.''
>But as he does not do any business
>he will never start.
They were like a farmer
who says:
''I haven't sufficient seed
to sow all my land;
wait till I have some more
and I will start.''
But as he does not sow the seed he has
he will never get any more seed
and he will go hungry.
>The disciples came to Jesus
>and they asked:
>''Give us some more faith
>and we will work wonders,''
>implying that
>at that moment their faith
>was too little,
>they couldn't do a thing.
Jesus, in a sense,
does not listen to their request
at all.
He does not promise them
any more faith.
He does not pledge them
anything at all.
Jesus said:
''Even if your faith
would be very small,
smaller than the smallest seed,
you would be able
to move mountains,

to move trees,
to move that tree over there,"
and he pointed at a mulberry tree,
a tree famous for its age
—it can become more than 600 years old—
and its very tenacious rooting system
that can break rocks
into pieces.
    Jesus just said:
    "Start with the little
    you have
    and you will work
    all you want."
He unmasked in them,
and he unmasked in us,
one of the ways
we use
to escape
our responsibilities:
    we can't pray
    because we haven't sufficient faith;
    we can't be charitable
    because we are very weak Christians;
    we can't organize ourselves in view of justice
    because we are only beginners;
    we can't stop drinking
    because we haven't sufficient grace. . . .
Jesus objected:
"Don't kid yourselves;
don't speak like that;
don't even ask for more,
but start with what you have!"
    Some years ago a lady died
    who was considered by very many
    a living saint.
    Her name was
    Dorothy Day.
    She started all kinds of activities,
    a newspaper, *The Catholic Worker,*
    that still exists;

houses of hospitality for vagrants
that still function;
feeding programs;
Christian communal farms;
et cetera.
Very many admirers
came to visit her,
to have a look at her,
to cherish her,
to speak to her,
to touch her, if possible.
Sometimes they would tell her:
"You are a saint";
or she would overhear others
saying of her:
"She is a saint."
She would turn to the speaker
and say:

 "Don't say that;
 don't make it so easy for yourself;
 don't escape in this way.
 I know why you are saying:
 'She is a saint.'
 You say that
 to convince yourself
 that you are different from me,
 that I am different from you.
 That is easy.
 In that case you can go
 your own way.

  I am not different from you;
  I am not a saint;
  I am like you.
  You could easily do
  what I do.
  You don't need any more faith
  than you have.
  Get kicking,
  Please."
  Amen.

47.

HE WAS AMAZED

2 Kings 5:14–17
2 Timothy 2:8–13
Luke 17:11–19

He was walking
in the border region
between Galilee and Samaria,
the region where the differences
between Jews and Samaritans
were most bitterly felt.
    A group of lepers
    came to ask his help,
    nine Jews and
    one Samaritan.
They remained at a distance
when they shouted at him
with their hands before their mouths,
as prescribed by the law.
    He did not approach them;
    he did not go to touch them;
    he told them from a distance
    to show themselves to the priests
    as, according to that same law,
    only priests could declare
    someone healed.

When he said this,
all in that strange group of people
turned around.
It was a strange group
not only because they were all sick,
but also
because it was composed of people
who normally
would never be together:
>   nine Jews and
>   one Samaritan!
>   Jews and Samaritans
>   did not live together;
>   they did not pray together;
>   they did not communicate with each other,
>   not ever.
Those ten were together
because they had been expelled,
all ten of them,
from their communities.
They were together
because they were all sick;
they were together
because they were all miserable;
they were together
because they were all
on their way
to death.
>   Before,
>   they had been discriminating;
>   before,
>   they had been discussing
>   each other's inferiority;
>   before,
>   they had been despising each other;
>   before,
>   they had never been seen together,
>   but all that had stopped
>   when fate
>   had swept them together

into that pitiful heap
of ten.
It is something that happens
so often in life.
Disaster strikes
and barriers are broken.
    In a bus
    where people were sitting silently aloof,
    not willing to talk
    because of their differences
    in class and color,
    in dress and odor,
    suddenly everything changes
    when the bus gets in an accident
    and overturns
    and people scramble out
    holding each other's hands.
In a university
a sudden disaster
brings together those
who even refused to shake hands
or eat at the same table
before.
    During war
    danger unites leaders and people,
    the rich and the poor.
In human history
proletarians from all over the world
come together
in a united front
because of the dangers
ahead.
    In a family
    brothers and sisters
    who had been fighting
    like mad
    sit together
    around the deathbed
    of the mother
    they all love.

The ten had turned around
on their way to the priests,
and first one,
then the second one,
the third one,
and the fourth . . .
each in turn
felt healed
and healthy
in a tight,
new, taut skin.
They looked at each other.
Their misery was over
and immediately
they split,
the nine and the one,
the Jews and the Samaritan—
the Samaritan
who in fact could not even go
with those Jews
to their priests in Jerusalem.
>   They had been together
>   on their way to death;
>   they could not be together
>   on their way to life.
>   Even Jesus was amazed,
>   and he said:
>   "You were ten.
>   Where are the others?"
>   It was that amazement
>   that made him
>   bring us
>   —commemorating him
>   during this meal—
>   together
>   on our way
>   to
>   life.
>   Let it be.
>   Oh, let it be.

48.

SATURATION PRAYER

Exodus 17:8–13
2 Timothy 3:14–4:2
Luke 18:1–8

Our prayers to God
often seem to be heard
by ourselves.
While Moses asked God
for a victory
over what he considered to be
the evil in this world,
his soldiers fought that victory.
> The widow in the gospel
> must have prayed to God
> that *the judge*
> would hear her prayer.
Take the student
who is praying for success in his examinations:
isn't he praying
that he himself may succeed;
isn't he praying
that he may spend the necessary time
behind his desk;
isn't he praying
that he may use the techniques needed

to retain what he studied
and to reproduce
what he knows?
    Think about that sick person
    who has to undergo
    a serious operation:
    when she, and her surgeon,
    her family, and the nurses
    pray for a successful operation,
    isn't that prayer
    going to be heard
    by their attention
    and care.
Or take that other life-issue
for which so many people
are praying at the moment
all over the world:
the end of the armaments race,
disarmament,
and peace in the world.
    There are going to be more and more
    peace demonstrations
    chanting peace slogans;
    missile sites
    will be more and more
    surrounded by people
    who pray
    to have those missiles removed.
    Don't you think,
    that if all the people
    in the world
    were to pray seriously
    for peace,
    those prayers
    would be heard?
    Don't you think
    that if all the people
    in the world
    were to pray seriously
    for an end to the armaments race,

 that race would
 stop?
In the gospel of today
Jesus speaks about the necessary
consistency
in prayer,
about the necessary
insistency.
He explains
how prayer works;
he explains
how prayer is heard.
 The widow
 who wanted justice done to her
 went again and again
 to the judge
 who despised her
 and who did not want to help her
 as she was poor and uninfluential.
 She kept coming,
 once a day,
 twice a day,
 three times a day,
 for one week,
 for a second week,
 for a third week,
 for a fourth week,
 filling the mind of that judge
 —though unjust—
 with the idea
 that justice
 should be done
 to her.
 She added every day
 a new reason.
 She showed every day
 a new aspect
 up to the moment
 that the head of that judge
 was totally oversaturated

with the thought
of her,
up to the moment
that he only thought of her
when waking up
in the morning,
up to the moment
that he decided
to do her the justice
she wanted
and deserved.
It works
like that glass of water
in which you start
to dissolve sugar.
You add one spoon of sugar,
you stir,
the sugar dissolves;
you add more sugar,
you stir,
the sugar dissolves;
you again add more sugar,
you stir,
it dissolves
up to the point
that the water gets oversaturated;
it cannot hold any more sugar
and it is at that point
that you have to add
only one more grain,
the smallest crystal of sugar possible,
to have the whole situation change,
and suddenly
all the sugar
crystalizes out of the water
in one abrupt movement.
This is what will happen
if we pray enough
for the real issues
of our times.

The issues that,
if solved,
will hear and solve
so many of our more personal prayers
for our own employment,
for our own health,
for our own family,
for our own food,
for our own drink,
for our own career.
> This is what will happen
> if we, all of us, raise
> our hands high enough
> and long enough,
> praying for justice,
>> for peace,
>> for unity,
>> for love.

Praying like that,
we are saturating
our minds and our spirits
with those divine desires,
more and more,
up to the moment
that we will be
suddenly
heard
by ourselves
with the help of God.
> That is how it will work.
> That is what Jesus tells us today,
> but he adds
> a warning too:
> Will this growing faith
> be found
> on this earth?

It should be
till the end.

49.

ON CHURCH GOING

Ecclesiastes 35:12–14, 16–19
2 Timothy 4:6–8, 16–18
Luke 18:9–14

The story Jesus told
is about us;
it is about people
who go to church.
    Luke gave this story an introduction;
    he gave it an intention.
    Luke says that Jesus told it
    because some glorified in their justice
    and therefore despised others.
    Because of Luke's preface
    we run the risk of being biased
    when listening to Jesus' parable.
    Because of Luke's introduction
    we will condemn the Pharisee
    as a hypocrite
    even before we have heard
    the end of Jesus' story.
    Modern commentators tell us
    to listen to the story
    without taking into account
    Luke's use of it.

The story
is about us
here in church today
and it is about those
who did not come.
Very many people
did not come,
including very many students.
If they all had come
we would number over 6,000
but we number
only about 1,100.

      Those who did not come
      often harass us
      for having come.
      Some days ago
      the University Young Christian Students Association
      had a meeting.
      In that meeting
      this kind of accusation
      could be heard.
      Someone said:
      "People go to church
      with very pious faces,
      a Bible under their left arm,
      a hymnal under their right arm;
      they sing alleluias
      with high pitched, excited voices;
      they receive holy communion
      very devotedly;
      but
      they are hypocrites
      because as soon as they are
      out of church
      they forget all about what they did
      in that church.
      As soon as it is Monday
      they will be bribing
      in their work again;

they will be corrupt
and faithless;
they will be just like all the others;
they will be just like us
who never go to church
because we don't want to join
their fake games.''
Have you ever been told
that you are a hypocrite
because you go to church?
In how many homes
did the husband stay in bed
this very morning
while his wife was preparing
to go to church?
And while she was putting on her
Sunday dress,
while she was arranging her
Sunday hat,
while she was looking for the Bible
that got lost during the confusion
of the week,   ·
he said from that bed:
    ''There she goes
    with her Bible and her hat,
    with her piety and her pretense!
    Hypocrite,
    don't you remember
    how you behaved
    over the last week,
    how you gossiped and slandered,
    how you nagged and lied?
    Hypocrite,
    I am not going to join you
    in that game,
    in that show,
    in that spectacle,''
    and he turned over
    to go back to sleep.

How often
have we read
in letters to the editors:
"All Christians are hypocrites.
They are pretenders."
How often do people say:
"Church-goers are no better
than those who don't go.
In fact, they are worse.
They are pious frauds,
Pharisees."
    All this implies
    that only the holy ones
    should go to church:
    the totally honest,
    the totally chaste,
    the totally sincere,
    those in whom there is nothing
    but goodness,
    and fairness,
    and divine beauty,
    those who,
    in fact,
    don't need God's mercy
    or help at all.
Jesus told them a story
about two people
who went to the temple.
They were two
different persons.
One was good,
sincerely good,
in a way even too good.
    He never robbed;
    he never treated anyone injustly;
    he never broke the sixth commandment;
    he fasted 104 days a year,
    though only one day was prescribed;
    he paid church tax on everything,

> though he only had to do it
> on cereals, oil, and wine.

This man was so holy
that he definitely
could go to church;
he belonged there;
he was no hypocrite;
he lived up to his ideal.

> In the back of the temple
> there is that other one,
> a tax collector,
> robbing,
> very unjust,
> greedy,
> adulterous,
> a man
> who should *never* have gone
> to a church.
> The hypocrite!
> What was he doing there?
> Who did he think he was?
> Out!

Jesus did not judge like that;
Jesus listened to his prayer;
and Jesus recognized
how his prayer started
with the beginning verse
of Psalm 51:

> "Be merciful to me, O God,
> because of your constant love.
> Because of your great mercy
> wipe away my sins!
> Wash away all my evil
> and make me clean from my sin!
> I recognize my faults;
> I am always conscious of my sins.
> I have sinned against you
> —only against you—
> and done what you consider evil.

So you are right in judging me;
you are justified in condemning me.
I have been evil from the time I was born;
from the day of my birth I have been sinful.
Sincerity and truth are what you require;
fill my mind with your wisdom.
Remove my sin, and I will be clean;
wash me, and I will be whiter than snow.
Let me hear the sounds of joy and gladness;
and though you have crushed me and broken me,
I will be happy once again.
Close your eyes to my sins
and wipe out all my evil.
Create a pure heart in me, O God,
and put a new and loyal spirit in me.
Do not banish me from your presence;
do not take your spirit away from me.
Give me again the joy that comes from
your salvation,
and make me willing to obey you.''
How could a man praying like that
be called a hypocrite?
Jesus did not do that either;
Jesus did not say
that he should not be in the temple;
on the contrary,
Jesus said:
''This man went home
a better man;
he went home,
changed and
justified.''
    If we prayed in this way,
    who would be able
    to call us hypocrites
    and should not those remaining home,
    because they think us hypocrites,
    and themselves sinners,
    join too?

50.

LOVER OF LIFE

Wisdom 11:22–12:2
2 Thessalonians 1:11–2:2
Luke 19:1–10

Zaccheus was bad;
he was convinced of that
himself.
It was a conviction
strengthened by the others
around him.

    He was a tax collector;
    he was corrupt,
    he was rich,
    and he was small.
No wonder
that he could not get
through the crowd
to see Jesus.
Every time he tried
others were putting their elbows
on his shoulders
without even noticing
what they did.

And when they noticed it
because he gave a shout,
they looked down at him
and said,
"What are you doing here?
This is no place for you."
And they would push him
again
to the outside of the circle
people were forming
around
Jesus.

    Zaccheus gave up,
    reconsidered his case,
    saw some boys
    who had climbed a tree,
    and he hastened
    —an extraordinary activity
    for a rich man like him—
    to a tree
    and climbed in it,
    sitting next to some birds
    in between heaven and earth.
Jesus and the crowd
milling around him
arrived under the tree.
Jesus stopped,
looked up,
and while all the others looked up too,
he said:
"Zaccheus, come down quickly.
I want to be your guest."
And Zaccheus hastened down,
and received him gladly.

    But the others started to murmur
    and said:
    "How can he do a thing like that?
    Doesn't he know
    that the man is no good?

Doesn't he know
that the food on his table
is stolen from our tables?
Doesn't he know
that the drinks in his cellar
are, so to speak,
our sweat and our blood?"
They all said that
Zaccheus is a sinner,
and Jesus agreed.
There is no doubt
about that.
They all said that
Zaccheus is no good,
but it was on this
that Jesus disagreed.

Zaccheus was a sinner;
his ethical life was no good,
his morals lousy,
his decisions in life wrong,
his relationships defective,
but to say
that he was no good
at all was impossible
for Jesus
who knew
that Zaccheus
had been created
by his Father.
There was a goodness
in Zaccheus
that nobody would be able
to take away;
there was a goodness
in Zaccheus
that was placed there by God,
our creator.

Didn't our first reading of today
from the book of Wisdom read:

"You love all that exists,
you hate nothing
of what you have created,
because
if you had hated it,
you would not have created it.
You, *lover of life*."
It is this goodness
that will never be
undone;
it is this goodness
Jesus came to reveal
in Zaccheus,
and in us.
We should never forget
this goodness
that will last
as long
as human life lasts.
It is this positive good
Jesus found in Zaccheus
that was provoked,
called up
and stimulated
by him.
It is this positive good
in and around us
we should provoke,
call up,
and stimulate.
If we only stress the negative,
that goodness might get
lost,
but not in the sense
that it will be
no longer
there.
A lost key
is still there,

> but we don't know
> where;
> a lost identity card
> is still there,
> but we don't know
> where;
> some lost money
> is still there,
> but we forgot
> where.

Jesus came
to find this goodness,
and once found
it blossomed
immediately
in Zaccheus.

> While they were sitting
> at table,
> Jesus took a piece
> of roasted lamb,
> but bringing it to his mouth
> he must have hesitated.
> Wasn't he eating
> from the table of the poor?
> Wasn't he dealing
> in stolen goods?
> Zaccheus
> saw his hesitation;
> he understood it
> and he said:
> "I will repay
> all the injustices I did;
> you can eat in peace."

That is
what Jesus did,
who had come
to find
what was lost.

51.

THE RESURRECTION OF
OUR BODIES

2 Maccabees 7:1-2, 9-14
2 Thessalonians 2:16-3:5
Luke 20:27-38

You all know
how sad it is
when a person dies
without leaving children,
without leaving a daughter,
without leaving a son.
 In more traditional contexts
 it means disaster,
 utter disaster.
 Who is going to remember
 that boy of fifteen
 who died before having been able to marry,
 before any new life had been born to him?
 He is going to be forgotten
 very soon;
 he is going to lose contact with life
 within a very short time
 after the death of his father,

after the death of his mother,
after the memory
of his sisters and brothers
fade away.
Disaster,
utter disaster.
That is what one thought
in the old days of Moses,
and that is why Moses
had given them the law
that Sadducees speak about
to Jesus
in the gospel of today.

Moses had stipulated
that if a man died
without having given life to his wife,
his brother
should get her with child
for her husband
who died.

It was the only way in which
people in that time
could visualize
life after death:
a life lasting
as long as you are remembered
by those around you,
by those left by you
in this world.

For the same reason
others sometimes built
enormous monuments,
like the pyramids in Egypt,
during their lives,
to be remembered
forever after.

But, of course, one day
you would be forgotten;

one day the history of others
would eat and digest you;
one day even the largest monument
would turn into dust;
you would be nowhere anymore
because you depended on those
who in their turn
would disappear too.
       That is what Moses thought;
       that is what the Sadducees thought;
       but another idea
       had been growing slowly,
       the idea believed by the Pharisees
       of the gospel of today,
       the idea that everyone
       would rise from the dead,
       the idea
       that the life of no one would end,
       that all would remain alive.
Hadn't the prophets said,
in the name of the almighty God:
"Even if a mother,
suckling her baby at her breast,
is able to forget about her child,
a rather impossible thing anyhow,
I, your God, will never forget you"?
Hadn't the prophets written,
in the name of the almighty God:
"I have written your name
on the palm of my hand"?
       It is the belief
       we express in our creed;
       it is what Jesus believed;
       it was what happened to him
       when he rose from the dead.
In our myths
heroes very often
overcame death

by hitting on the mystery of life,
by brewing an eternal life elixir,
by eating from the old tree of life,
by swallowing a pearl,
by taking a miraculous bath.
>   Jesus did not overcome death
>   like that;
>   he did it
>   by letting himself be loved by God
>   unconditionally.
That is what we should do,
let ourselves be loved by God
unconditionally.
>   But how do we know,
>   how did Jesus know,
>   that God loves us?
John answered that question
several times
in his gospel
and in his letters.
>   *We know*
>   *that God loves us,*
>   *because we love others!*
In a research project in the United States
in 1972,
Catholic priests were asked
whether they ever had
any religious experience
in their lives.
Fifty-six percent answered
yes;
and twenty-five percent
spoke about mystical experiences;
they felt sometimes
one-with-God.
>   The researchers tried to find
>   some correlations.
>   Which priests had those experiences,
>   and for what reasons?

First they thought
it would be the priests
with a very strong prayer life,
but they discovered
that there was no correlation
with any type of spiritual exercises.
The only correlation
found
was their attitude
to the people around them.
The priests who related well
to the community
around them,
the priests who were loving,
welcoming, and outgoing,
were the ones with those
religious and spiritual experiences.
We express this ourselves
in a very nice way
in our creed
when we say:
"We believe in the resurrection of the body
and eternal life."
In that order:
first the body
then the life.
We were created for others;
our bodies show that,
our faces especially.
Did you ever see
your own face?
You never did.
Even if you look
in a mirror
you don't see your face
as it is.
You see it distorted,
the right at the left
and the left at the right.

Our faces are not created
to be seen by ourselves;
our faces are created
to be seen by others.
Our bodies are created
in the direction of
the others.
We are made
towards them.
In the end
we will be saved
in that way.
God who loves all of us
loves each one of us
in as far as we love
those others;
and it is in this way
that we find our reason
to believe
in eternal life,
because of the resurrection
of our bodies,
because of the resurrection
of Jesus Christ.

52.

THE COMING END

Malachi 3:19–20
2 Thessalonians 3:7–12
Luke 21:5–19

When they thought about the end,
they thought about a sudden crash;
when they thought about the end,
they thought about something
that would happen
very suddenly, in the wink of an eye,
and all at once.
Many of us still do;
yet is that what he wanted them to believe
in the gospel of today?
 Once an angel was sent by God to a village,
 to a group of houses scattered
 through the countryside.
 The angel was sent
 to the families in that place
 with one and the same message:
 "I am he,
 the time has come."
In all the homesteads
the angel visited,
people had been praying
for one or another intention,

like we are all
praying and hoping
for something,
aren't we?
        In the first house
        the angel visited,
        a boy of about ten
        had been praying
        for a pair of shoes.
        He had no shoes;
        everyone else in school had shoes,
        but he hadn't.
        His father and his mother,
        his uncles and his aunts,
        his grandfathers and his grandmothers
        were too poor to buy him shoes,
        and he had been praying,
        praying for weeks and weeks:
        "Shoes, God, please, shoes."
        When the angel knocked at the door,
        it was the boy who opened,
        and when the angel said,
        "I am he,
        the time has come,"
        the boy looked immediately at his feet,
        shod in beautiful leather boots.
In the second house
a very old man
had been waiting for his death
for quite some time.
They said he was over a hundred.
It was already very long ago
that he had called his children,
his sons and his daughters,
to divide his estate,
to arrange the last things,
but he had never died.
He prayed every day:
"Oh, God, come and fetch me.

I want to join my ancestors.
Please let me go,"
but it had all been in vain.
He got older and older,
and he felt more and more pain
every day.
When the angel knocked at his door,
he saw him from his bed,
and when he heard the angel say,
"I am he,
the time has come,"
he stretched his limbs on that bed
for the last time
and died in the Lord,
saying,
"Thanks be to God."
     In the third house
     a firm, young woman
     was overdue,
     expecting her first child
     that would not come.
     Her neighbors had warned her
     that if it did not come quickly
     she would be in trouble,
     and she had been praying
     "Oh, God, let it come.
     Don't let it wait
     any longer."
     When the angel knocked on her door,
     she moved with great difficulty
     from her stool,
     heavy as she was,
     but when she heard his message,
     "I am he,
     the time has come,"
     she felt the baby come.
Brothers and sisters,
I told you this story to show
that if such a message comes,

"I am he,
the time has come,"
so much depends
on what people expect.
       In the story of today
       Jesus speaks about the end
       of this world,
       about the moment
       that he will come to say,
       "I am he,
       the time has come."
It is obvious from the gospel
what the contemporaries of Jesus thought
would happen that day:
the sky would fall,
the sun would burst,
the moon would disintegrate,
there would be a sudden change,
all at once,
a total instantaneous overhaul,
the end of all that was old.
You must have heard often enough
descriptions of this
by the prophets of doom.
       But we should not forget
       that those people
       lived in a time
       when things moved very slowly,
       if they moved at all;
       for hundreds of years
       things had remained the same;
       they had been hoeing with hoes
       that had not changed
       for thousands of years;
       they had been living
       oppressed by others endlessly.
       The idea of history,
       of development, and progress,
       hardly existed;

and that is why,
when they thought of change,
a real change,
they could think only
of one big bang,
one enormous crunch,
something sudden
and fast.
They saw no other possibility.
For us things have changed;
we live in other times;
we know about development;
many things have been changing
around us over the last fifty years:
radios and cars,
telephones and television,
tools and computers,
political systems and economies.
When we hear
the message of Jesus,
"I am he,
the time has come,"
we might think,
we even should think,
in terms
of a growth
that is taking place
already,
in terms of the development
we see all around us.
The end will come
that is sure;
and it is certain
because Jesus announced:
the seed has been planted,
the light has been lit,
the yeast is in the dough,
the salt is in the world,
the end is going to come.

This implies
that we have to cooperate.
It means
that we cannot sit down
as the Christians did
to whom Paul wrote.
They had, in view of the end,
stopped work.
>We have to hasten the process
>of which Jesus said:
>"You can't really observe
>the coming of the Kingdom.
>It is coming
>slowly."
We, in our world,
we, in our church,
are not accustomed
to that slowness.
We don't want to wait;
we are too masculine;
we are too aggressive;
everything has to come
in one quick rush,
the way a man
helps to create a new life.
We are not sufficiently female,
we are not sufficiently
motherly,
waiting for nine long months
with growing joy,
until new life is born.
>So much
>has still
>to change.
>We are far
>from the end.

53.

KINGDOM SEEN

2 Samuel 5:1–3
Colossians 1:12–20
Luke 23:35–43

It was a very sad group of people
going to the execution place
that afternoon:
Jesus,
two criminals,
police, soldiers,
and their assistants.
It was a very glad group of people too,
the priests, the scribes,
the dignitaries, and magistrates
who had him condemned to death.
Then there was the crowd
that so easily assembles
on such occasions.
> The group was even more sad
> once they were hanging on their crosses,
> Jesus in the middle,
> the two robbers on both sides,
> one on the right,
> the other one on the left.

257

In conformity with
the prevailing regulations,
the reason for their condemnation
was mentioned above their heads.
The inscription above the man
on his right read:
robbery with violence.
The inscription above the man
on his left read:
robbery with violence.
The one above his own head read:
Jesus, King of the Jews.
The priests were laughing at him;
they paid no attention
to the two others;
they were not interested in them;
they were there only
to see Jesus die,
the man who had threatened
their set-up
and their income.
The people were just standing there;
they were looking at the three,
but they too looked especially at
Jesus.

There was no trace of beauty
in him
anymore;
he had been mangled too badly
during the last twenty-four hours
since his arrest.
The priests had given up on him
long ago;
the people were doing that now;
after his death,
they would go home
in utter silence,
beating their chests
in horror and despair.

They could not see any good
anymore
in the one
who had not stopped
seeing good,
a trace of divinity,
a trace of God's kingdom,
in all of them,
even in the smallest,
    the poorest,
    the most sinful,
    the most terribly handicapped,
    the ones screaming
    with all kinds of evil spirits
    in themselves.
Hadn't he been the one who,
when that prostitute came in
and everyone said,
"She is very bad,
a real sinner,"
said:
"There is some good in her;
one will speak about her
until the end of time
because of that
goodness in her!"
    Hadn't he been the one who,
    when Zaccheus hid in the tree,
    convinced of his sinfulness,
    called him down from that tree,
    saying:
    "Zaccheus, don't be silly,
    come down.
    You too are the son of Abraham.
    I want you to be my host.
    I want to be your guest!"
Now death reigned;
evil seemed to have overcome;
hope was definitely squashed;

God seemed to be absent.
Did he himself not shout:
"My God, my God,
why have you forsaken me?"
>The priests started to jeer.
>They shouted:
>"Let God help you.
>Where is your God?"
>The soldiers joined them
>in their cheap fun.
>Even the robber on his left did the same.
Now the sun started to disappear.
Dark clouds gathered
between the cross and the sun,
that source of light to the world.
It became darker and darker;
people had to light torches
to see one another,
though it must have been
about three o'clock in the afternoon.
The earth started to tremble
as if in despair,
and no voice,
no voice
was heard from above.
A darker scene
had never been observed.
>And when all hope
>seemed to have gone,
>the one on the cross at his right
>looked up at him,
>*God only knows why*
>—was it the answer to his cry?
>And looking up
>he said:
>>"I see some kingdom in you.
>>I see some divinity in you.
>>I see some light in you.
>>I see some hope in you.

> I see some humanity in you.
> Please,
> when you arrive in your kingdom
> think of me!"
And Jesus lifted his head;
he looked up at the only one
who at that moment saw something
in him,
and he said:
>> "Of course
>> there is a kingdom;
>> of course
>> you will be there with me,
>> today!"
Brothers and sisters,
it sometimes seems
that all is very bad,
that everything is turned against us,
that all is dark,
that there is no hope.
The older you are,
the more you must have experienced this
already in your lives.
> Light is gone;
> darkness reigns;
> death looms;
> our enemies are laughing at us;
> we have shouted in vain
> for the Father
> to come.
Let us pray
that we always may find
someone to tell us
what the good murderer told Jesus:
"I see some kingdom in you.
I see some divinity in you.
I see some light in you.
I see some hope in you.
I see some humanity in you!"

Those words meant salvation to him;
they meant salvation to Jesus too,
the foundation of the kingdom
he started
together with that robber
that very day.
Let him reign
together with us
for all time
to come.
The good murderer
found
what seemed lost.
He did
what Jesus had done
all his life.
Hope
drawing near!

INDEX OF SCRIPTURAL TEXTS

OLD TESTAMENT